Alive in the Writing

Kirin Narayan

Alive IN THE *Writing*

CRAFTING ETHNOGRAPHY IN THE COMPANY OF CHEKHOV

The University of Chicago Press
CHICAGO AND LONDON

KIRIN NARAYAN is the author of *Storytellers, Saints, and Scoundrels*, *Mondays on the Dark Night of the Moon*, the novel *Love, Stars, and All That*, and the memoir *My Family and Other Saints*, also published by the University of Chicago Press. A former Guggenheim fellow, she is professor of anthropology at the University of Wisconsin–Madison.

The University of Chicago Press, Chicago 60637
The University of Chicago Press, Ltd., London

Printed in the United States of America

21 20 19 18 17 16 15 14 13 12   1 2 3 4 5

ISBN-13: 978-0-226-56818-8 (cloth)
ISBN-13: 978-0-226-56819-5 (paper)
ISBN-10: 0-226-56818-0 (cloth)
ISBN-10: 0-226-56819-9 (paper)

Library of Congress Cataloging-in-Publication Data

Narayan, Kirin.
Alive in the writing : crafting ethnography in the company of Chekhov / Kirin Narayan.
p. cm.
Includes bibliographical references and index.
ISBN-13: 978-0-226-56818-8 (alk. paper)
ISBN-10: 0-226-56818-0 (alk. paper)
ISBN-13: 978-0-226-56819-5 (pbk. : alk. paper)
ISBN-10: 0-226-56819-9 (pbk. : alk. paper)
1. Ethnology—Authorship. 2. Creative nonfiction—Authorship. 3. Chekhov, Anton Pavlovich, 1860–1904—Criticism and interpretation. 4. Ethnology in literature. I. Title.
GN307.7.N37 2012
305.8—dc23

2011023619

♾ This paper meets the requirements of ANSI/NISO Z39.48-1992 (Permanence of Paper).

In memory of two grandmothers—
Alice Marie Fish Kinzinger
who taught me how to read,
to write
and to find pleasure in crafting words

and

Kamlabai Ramji
who never read, never wrote,
and who confidently flung words
into the bright colors of stories

Of Chekhov Tolstoi said:

"He is a strange writer: he throws words about as if at random, and yet everything is alive. And what understanding! He never has any superfluous details; every one of them is either necessary or beautiful."

A. B. Goldenveizer, *Talks with Tolstoi*

Contents

PREFACE *Alive in the Writing*

When words gather together with energy, other places, other people, and other voices stir in a parallel life. The writer can feel more alive too, alert and connected to a welling inner source that flows outward toward other lives. This at least is the ideal. But words sometimes refuse to be summoned, leaving a writer sluggish and adrift, or worse, alone and depressed. To find inspiration, purpose, and nurturing company, a writer might look around for a writing group, a workshop, a class, or even a book like this: a book about writing.

I found the seeds for this book at the crossroads of ethnographic writing and creative nonfiction. As a cultural anthropologist and folklorist, I have for years been reading, writing, and teaching ethnographies—accounts that closely document and try to gain insight into people's lives as they unfold in particular situations and corners of the world. Since I was interested in writing itself, I also began teaching classes and workshops about writing ethnography. Ethnography is usually written as the result of a defined research project. Yet in the unfolding of everyday life we are all constantly considering—consciously and unconsciously—the complex ways that individual stories are entangled with social processes.

Long before I began writing ethnography, I was writing stories. I went on to also write novels and a family memoir. Moving between these forms, I began to reflect on the ways that life's raw materials can be shaped into absorbing stories that might not be labeled ethnography but are still ethnographically informed. And so, I started learning more about creative nonfiction: accounts based on actual people, places, and events, and written as imaginatively engaging stories. Creative nonfiction overlaps with such genres as personal essays, memoirs, biographies, nature writing, travel writing, literary journalism, and cultural criticism; in this book I also explore the ways it might intersect with ethnography.

You can find many useful books about ethnography as a research method or ethnography as a genre to be interpreted and theorized. Books that share practical strategies for generating and crafting ethnographic prose are rarer. This book is a hands-on guide, offering what I hope will be galvanizing examples and suggestions—though not prescriptions—for writers of ethnographic and ethnographically informed prose. My husband Ken playfully describes this book to friends as "not a *how-to* manual but a *how-about?* manual."

Some of what I share in this book, I learned from my dear friend Joanne Mulcahy, an inspired writer and teacher of writing who also works at the intersection of ethnography, folklore, and creative nonfiction. When I first taught ethnographic writing classes, I issued short assignments. But after offering a three-day workshop at Joanne's invitation, I learned to name the strategy that the theorist and teacher of writing Peter Elbow has popularized as *freewriting*—just writing forward, without judgment or concern for a polished product. I also learned the galvanizing use of *prompts*, specific examples or opening phrases that can help a writer bypass hovering hesitation over how or where to begin. I learned the power of writing together, whether in a class, a workshop, or just with a friend. And I learned the value in asking readers in advance for the sort of comments that would be most helpful at a given stage.

The process of writing invariably brings discoveries. Working on this book, my biggest surprise was finding myself apprenticed to Anton Chekhov, the Russian short story writer and playwright. Chekhov walked into my manuscript about fifty pages into the first draft, when a friend recommended I consider the ethnographic aspects of his 1895 book *Sakhalin Island*—a nonfiction account of the suffering and absurdities in the tsarist penal colony on Sakhalin, off the east coast of Russia, just north of Japan. I was curious: how might this work—which wasn't *cast* as ethnography but was nonetheless richly ethnographic— shed light on the contemporary projects of writing ethnography, whether for specialists or a general audience? Chekhov had trained as a doctor, and I became interested in how he combined empirical precision with an artist's evocative skill. I was compelled to read more about this dark-haired, bearded young man. Though he was already showing unacknowledged signs of tuberculosis, why had he left behind his family, friends, and fans to set off on a difficult journey across Siberia to Sakhalin? Tagging along after Chekhov, I found myself on an uncharted adventure that came to direct my route through subsequent chapters.

Chekhov has left behind a huge corpus of writing in addition to *Sakhalin Island*: almost six hundred stories of varied length, more than five thousand extant letters, four major plays and several minor ones, and a notebook. He also has inspired many reminiscences, biographies, and critical studies. When I entered the labyrinth of these materials, I marveled that someone who died on a warm July night in 1904 could still seem so present. Reading work by and about Chekhov, I have often felt that I am communing with a live sensibility: not just a name hallowed with fusty greatness but a playful, sad, smart presence just nanometers away though always beyond tangible reach. Each time I have begun to consider him familiar, some phrase or insight leaps from a page with such incandescence that I once again step back in awe. Sometimes my admiration has tilted toward veneration. But then I am uncomfortably reminded of ways that he was after all human, imperfect, contradictory, and—even though he might seem so contemporary—partially moored in the attitudes of his times. Following Chekhov's path across the last decades of the nineteenth century and first years of the twentieth, I perceived how he mellowed, growing gentler as a person and deepening as a writer. Throughout, I've been reminded of the uncanny ways that people remain alive through their writings, and alive too in closely observed writings about them.

Writing offers the chance to cultivate an attentiveness to life itself, and to enhance perceptions with the precision of words. Writing also potentially communicates images and insights to unseen circles of readers. The writing exercises I offer here twist together the possibilities for an inward-facing cultivation of understanding and an outward-facing performance for readers. We all can continually improve our ability to describe with vivid accuracy, to lay out ideas with clarity, to make every word count. Writing composed with craft touches readers on several levels—intellectual, emotional, aesthetic—and the impact lingers longer than words dashed off. Whether in books, essays or articles, grant applications, reviews, letters of application, blogs, or editorials, well-chosen words gather the power to change others' minds and possibly the conditions of our own lives. At its best, strong writing can direct attention to suffering and injustice, deepen compassion and outrage, elaborate imaginative alternatives, and mobilize energies for action.

This book doesn't need to be read all at once or in sequence. You might want to simply dip in: browsing themes, reading extracts from others' writings, following Chekhov, choosing prompts, trying an exercise. You might start by reading the postscript that assembles tips on how to begin writing, how to keep writing through periods of self-doubt, and how to revise and work through drafts to the completion of a project. You might choose to work with the book in company, finding a congenial friend or two to write with. Or perhaps you will meet up with the book in a class and follow someone else's itinerary through these pages.

The boldface prompts throughout the text are meant to initiate freewriting—uninterrupted writing that grows from whatever that seed suggests to you, and that you might later edit and refine. The exercises at the ends of chapters, though, call for more polished pieces intended for others' eyes. For these exercises, I suggest just two double-spaced pages—not a line more—and here are my reasons. First, learning to write with brevity is a gift to overburdened readers, and especially if you're working as part of a group, a short piece is more likely to receive considered comments. Second, I believe that forcing oneself to be concise renews respect for language itself, for the weight of every word. (Later, folding in readers' comments, you can expand to whatever length seems best.)

This book is inherently incomplete. To welcome readers from many backgrounds and to keep these pages from becoming unwieldy, I've forced myself to hold back from elaborating on anthropology's history and the disciplinary debates that underlie certain representational choices. I have also left out many wonderful books by ethnographers and other writers whom I admire. I've limited myself to prompts from books rather than essays or articles, and usually to just one book per writer. Perhaps these omissions will stir readers to fill in the gaps, identify other topics to write about, and design more prompts.

Writing about writing to his older brother Alexander in 1886, Chekhov qualified his own views: "I'm writing you this as a reader with preferences of my own. I'm also writing so that you shouldn't feel lonely in your work. The loneliness of creation is a burdensome thing." This book too is shaped by my own preferences and the impulse to find company amid the often isolating and difficult aspects of writing. While I suggest possible routes, the creative destinations are in your hands.

Whatever the writing journey you might be embarking on, I hope that Chekhov, the literary ethnographers, and the ethnographically inclined nonfiction writers I have assembled here may bring you good company and luminous inspiration.

ONE Story and Theory

In Anton Chekhov's "My Life: A Provincial's Story," the narrator, Misail Poloznev, momentarily takes on the persona of an ethnographer. Idealistic Misail, who's in his mid-twenties, is from a rich and self-consciously respectable family in a provincial Russian town. After losing yet another office job and further infuriating his dour father, Misail moves out to live only off his own labor. He eventually finds a foothold with a team of housepainters. Town tradesmen and shopkeepers scorn him as a traitor to his class: when he walks the streets in shabby workmen's clothes, he's teased and abused, and people throw things at him. Those who'd once been his social equals mostly shun him, but Marya Viktorovna, the attractive blonde daughter of the local railway magnate, is intrigued. She invites Misail to her mansion and assures him that being rich and living off others is dull. Then she presses him to tell her more about housepainters: "What are they like? Funny?" Misail reports, "I began telling about housepainters but was abashed, being unaccustomed, and spoke like an ethnographer, gravely and ploddingly."

An intellectual young doctor who has also joined the party likewise recounts stories about workingmen, but with such drama—reeling, weeping, kneeling, lying on the floor—that Marya laughs until she cries. Next the doctor sings; then Marya impersonates singers and sketches her visitors in her album. Over dinner, Marya joins the doctor in drinking toasts to high ideals—"friendship, reason, progress, freedom"—laughing hysterically, while Misail looks on, noting all.

I had been finding an unexpected source of energy in Chekhov's writings for a few months when I met this passage. Encountering this characterization of an ethnographer, I laughed too: from the fun of disciplinary self-recognition, and from the extreme contrast embodied in the slapstick reenactments by the energetic doctor. The very question of whether housepainters are *funny* has an edge of parody: the young woman, bored silly in the provincial town, is looking above all for diversion, and she clearly isn't that interested in housepainters beyond Misail. No wonder earnest Misail feels his account is not compelling.

The word "ethnography"—like "anthropology" itself—is a term that appeared with the developing social sciences in the nineteenth century. "Ethno" is from *ethnos*, a group of people who share a way of life; "graphy" is tied to inscription, or writing. Originally intended to offer detailed accounts of other, culturally distinct ways of life, ethnography has been famously termed "writing culture." But travelers, missionaries, and colonial officers had also been writing about other cultures, and ethnography was from its very inception torn between contrary impulses: to present empirical observations gathered through specific methods and processed with theory, or to appeal to readers' imaginations with colorful stories. While ethnography attempts to represent life in particular settings, the related practice of *ethnology* places lived particulars in a comparative framework, theorizing concepts across contexts. (In an earlier translation of the passage I quoted, Misail speaks "like an ethnologist, gravely and tediously.")

Anton Chekhov knew ethnography at least partly through background research for his nonfiction book *Sakhalin Island*. He had himself gestured toward the two faces of ethnography before his departure for Sakhalin in 1890, when he described himself as having "scientific and literary purposes in mind." I dwell more on the ethnographic aspects of *Sakhalin Island* in chapter 2, "Place," but for the moment I want to pause at Misail Poloznev's perception that when he spoke seriously and tediously about a form of life, he sounded like an ethnographer. Certainly, ethnography can be written in dry, dense, and convoluted ways. But from the nineteenth century onward, there have also been ethnographers who have written in lively, engaging styles. Even as different national and institutional settings have shaped the central goals and perceived borders of ethnography, every generation of ethnographers has produced—and continues to nurture—some brilliant stylists and storytellers.

Ethnographies with literary panache are not uniformly celebrated in anthropological histories—sometimes they are, sometimes they aren't. But these have occasionally reached wide popular audiences and are regularly pulled out to hold the attention of undergraduates in introductory anthropology courses. In the pages ahead, I look for examples of ethnographic craft in these more literary, humanistic, and frequently feminist works. I also turn to books that aren't strictly ethnographies, or explicitly related to anthropology at all, but that I consider to be deeply ethnographic in their ability to vividly represent people within shared situations. Pressing beyond the tight exclusivity of "ethnography," then, I make room for what a writer might learn from the *ethnographic* aspects of other forms of writing.

Mostly I draw on nonfiction, though through Chekhov I touch on fiction too. So for example, while "My Life" is in no way a formal ethnography, the story is saturated with ethnographic insight about late nineteenth-century Russia. Even if Misail feels himself to have failed in offering a pretty woman an interesting account of his work, Chekhov's story *about* Misail reveals the quotidian handling of linseed oil, paint, and turpentine; the interchanges among men as they work together to paint the railway line, town club, and atmospheric cemetery church; and the demeaning rituals and mutual dishonesty in relationships with clients. Throughout the story Misail brings a wide-eyed perplexity to social worlds that he sees afresh after having shifted social positions. Following his travails, readers learn about the nobility's romantic fascination with the lives of peasants and laborers, about class structure, social inequality, gender relations, intellectual fads, small-town enthusiasms, and more. If Misail isn't literally taking notes, he is always noting what other people are saying and doing, and trying to figure out what this could mean. He discovers, close-up, the textures and rhythms of life among town laborers and, later, peasants in the countryside; simultaneously, he is forced to revise his views of upper-class people he once thought he understood. This dual movement of trying to grasp the exotic or unfamiliar while also reevaluating the familiar is of course key to the practice of ethnography.

In this chapter I offer a few writing exercises directed toward shaping a larger outcome from the smaller pieces of writing I suggest through the chapters ahead. I also present some very basic tools for composition, forged from an alloy of ethnography and creative nonfiction. As my mother said, pencil in hand, looking up from an earlier version of these pages, "It's not just a question of getting people going with their writing. A lot of people I know have no problem writing. The bigger thing I'd like to know is, do you have any thoughts on how to put all the different little bits together?"

Taking Stock

You might be working in the frame of a well-delineated research project that involves systematic methods for assembling data, presupposes particular questions, and participates in disciplinary conversations. For a formal ethnographic research project, one intended for publication, you will need to satisfy the human subject protocols required by universities and granting bodies, and become conversant with relevant literature. Alternately, you might be contemplating creative nonfiction that draws on your own memories and observations without an explicit scholarly apparatus, addressing an interested reader of no particular disciplinary affiliation. However you may be developing your materials, keep your intended audience or audiences in mind: you may need to defend your choices.

Before you begin writing in the company of this book, I suggest that you inventory the raw materials you hope to draw on. Bring out your older scribblings and writings, whether lodged in journals, letters, e-mails, blogs, finished pieces, drafts of grant proposals, or formal field notes. Also assemble nonwritten materials: photographs, videos, recordings, music. The very project of sorting and handling these raw or partly processed materials will reconnect you with them afresh. Organize these, so you know what's where when you need it: "piles to files," as a friend says. And if you have meticulously arranged your files, look through them to remind yourself of your full range of materials.

As you proceed through this book, freewriting from prompts or producing more polished two-page pieces from the exercises presented at the end of each chapter, continually ask yourself how you'd like all this to add up. What form do you envision? If you're writing within an institutional setting, you may be bound to a very particular form: a term paper, a conference paper, a dissertation, a journal article, a scholarly book. Depending on the immediate audience, you may be able to enliven and subvert a given form, but be attentive to what's expected of you; if necessary, protect your innovations by citing disciplinary precedents. You might allow the form to emerge from materials given to you by the people you seek to describe: their central metaphors and organizing principles. You might collaborate with those you are writing about to arrive at a form that will satisfy both your goals and theirs. Depending on your eventual goal, your work may be driven more by stories or by theories; larger contexts and ideas might remain tacit, or you might draw these into explicitly stated orientations and arguments, marked with citation and backed up by a bibliography. In his wonderful book that assembles fiction techniques to craft nonfiction, Theodore Rees Cheney observes that "creative nonfiction writers inform their readers by making the reading experience vivid, emotionally compelling, and enjoyable while sticking to the facts." Ethnographies can also be vivid, emotionally compelling and enjoyable, but if written within a conventional disciplinary frame they are also expected to be clearly argued, intellectually persuasive, and theoretically insightful.

Here, then, is my first prompt for a bout of freewriting. The instructions I offer are intended to help you start off and set your words moving; after this, just write forward without worrying about polish. Later you can look back, clarify, and rearrange. For the particularly broad and open-ended freewrites in this chapter, I suggest approximate times; in subsequent chapters I leave the times to you. If you feel unsure as you meet these prompts, blurry statements like "I'm not exactly sure" or "something about x" are fine; just keep writing. See where the flow of your own words takes you. I usually learn something I wasn't consciously aware of as I give form to diffuse ideas, feelings, and images through written words.

▹ Beginning with the words "I most hope to write . . ." write forward for at least 5 minutes.

Now reflect on what you wrote. Most likely, this turned out to be something very general. Trying to describe my intentions to myself, at different times I started with "a book about writing ethnographically, livened up by inspiring examples and practical exercises," "a book about writing that also introduces readers to Anton Chekhov," and even just "a book that will be useful, even if it is incomplete." Nothing too fancy, but each time the words became a compass offering a larger orientation and direction.

Now I ask you to move to particulars:

▹ Quickly write down a few images that jump out at you as you think of the materials you're drawing on for this undertaking. Continue for at least 5 minutes.

Here's an unpolished image that emerged for me as I thought of the writing classes and workshops that inspired this book: "rapt faces as participants listen to each others' comments, the sense of perfect attentiveness around tables laid out in a square, light falling through windows along one side of the room, my own listening, note taking, anxious tension over being properly present, and also thinking ahead on how to move the discussion forward . . ." Turning to images with concrete details can be a way of grounding yourself in the lived context of your undertaking. (Alternatively, if you started with specifics, move to the most general possible statement about what you hope to write.)

Also start imagining what a reader might make of your offering. I often think back to a letter written by J. D. Salinger's character Seymour Glass to his younger brother, Buddy, who wanted to be a writer. Seymour reminded Buddy that he'd already been a reader for a long time, and advised him to sit still, ask himself what he'd most *want to read*, and write just that. Try this. Think about your finished product, then step away, trying to imagine how you'd most appreciate meeting it as a reader.

▹ Beginning with the words "I'd most want to read . . ." write for at least 2 minutes.

Taking this perspective, I was immediately aware that I'd want "a book that was short, to the point, and energizing." You're likely to come up with different characterizations of your project at different times. Between very specific exercises, you may find it helpful to periodically revisit and refresh such statements of larger intent.

First Impressions

Looking back at the journey that led you to care about something can also be a way to get started. As I began working on this book, I thought again of what had inspired my orientation to ethnographic writing. I quickly list these as a way of offering tribute to mentors even as I reflect more on ethnography.

I first seriously settled into reading ethnographies as a freshman in college. I had glanced at popular anthropology paperbacks before that, but it was only when I signed up for a seminar taught by Irving Goldman that I closely read a sequence of ethnographies. In a quiet yet forceful way, Mr. Goldman (as we called him) taught us to read closely for cultural details. Rather than emphasizing a book's argument, we learned how new patterns and connections could emerge from paying attention to observed details and indigenous exegeses of their meaning. At the time, I had no intention of becoming an anthropologist, but cultural anthropology spoke powerfully to the many cultural influences in my background. I grew up in Bombay as a child of an American mother and Indian father. I found myself exploring aspects of this background in creative writing workshops and was especially drawn to the colloquial, unadorned style of my writing teacher Grace Paley.

I first thought about ethnography in relation to writing during my senior year. This was my second anthropology class, this time with Bradd Shore, who proved so inspiring and charismatic that my nebulous plans for graduate school took shape around anthropology. At some point in the semester, Bradd Shore assigned two essays from *The Interpretation of Cultures*, by the influential anthropologist and cultural critic Clifford Geertz. I was intrigued by what Geertz had to say about ethnography, not just as a means of recording different ways of life, but also as a form of writing. In the introductory essay Geertz characterizes ethnography as a form of "thick description." To use the example that he borrows from the philosopher Gilbert Ryle, thick description would tell you not just that someone's eye had contracted but whether the contraction was a twitch, a wink, a parody of a wink, a rehearsal for a parody of a wink, or a knowingly faked wink.

Layering meaning into closely observed details, thick description helps make people's behavior more comprehensible when we aren't immediately familiar with their assumptions.

I first thought about ethnography in relation to strategies of storytelling as a graduate student. In the classes of my generous advisor, the folklorist Alan Dundes, I learned to think about how stories carry personal and cultural meaning, and how their telling has social consequences. At the same time, Pauline Kolenda, a visiting professor, introduced me to different ways that ethnographers had theorized on South Asia. During my second year I made a weekly pilgrimage to Stanford, to sit in on a seminar called "Stories and Culture" taught by the cultural anthropologist Renato Rosaldo. With this class my delight in recording and interpreting oral narratives stretched toward understanding how narratives of all kinds—including those written by scholars are linked to social analysis. Rosaldo's *Culture and Truth: The Remaking of Social Analysis* (1989) argues the case at greater and more subtle length, but let me share two valuable things I learned from this class: that stories are incipiently analytic, and that in the sequence of reasoning, analysis has a narrative form.

▹ Sketch the first steps that brought you to your project, mentioning specific people or ideas. (5 minutes)

First impressions can shape lasting orientations, but these too can be refined and revised. As I've reread Geertz's essay "Thick Description: Toward an Interpretive Theory of Culture," I've also wondered: if we are writing as cultural insiders for others already in the know, how might thick description be offered without obvious interpretive asides, so that familiar worlds can emerge as newly strange and remarkable? How do we engage multiple audiences that increasingly include the very people being written about, or their close relatives? What one reader finds perplexing and opaque may be for a differently positioned reader a telling detail that, without a word of interpretation, lights up broad social distinctions. Generating narrative momentum can, I believe, thicken description not just through obvious exegesis, but also by following the consequences of actions and shifts in understanding on the part of various participants, including the writer.

In the same essay, Geertz also described ethnographic works as "fictions in the sense that they are 'something made,' 'something fashioned'—the original meaning of fiction—not that they are false, unfactual, or merely 'as if' thought experiments." Some years later, he reiterated this insight—that ethnographies are crafted representations, like fiction though not fictional: "It is not clear just what 'faction,' imaginative writing about real people in real places, exactly comes to beyond a clever coinage; but anthropology is going to have to find out if it is to continue as an intellectual force in contemporary culture." What Geertz calls "faction" is of course a sort of creative nonfiction. This brings me back to the building blocks of storytelling as conceived of by creative nonfiction writers.

Scenes, Summaries, Events

Writers of creative nonfiction distinguish between vivid, sensual *scenes*, complete with details, description, and dialogue, and *summaries* that afford more general overviews. The poet and memoirist Judith Barrington expresses the contrast in cinematic terms. For her, the scene is like "the close-up, the camera zooming in through the kitchen window, picking out the two figures talking at the table and going up really close to the face of first one speaker then the other while the audience hears one speak." The summary, on the other hand, is "the long shot . . . that pulls back to a great distance, embracing first the whole house, then the street, then the neighborhood, and then becoming an aerial shot, it takes in the whole city and maybe the surrounding mountains too." Summaries, then, situate a scene in broader frames of space and time, and condense large swaths of narrative action. Used together, the scenes enliven the summaries and the summaries connect up particular scenes.

The opening passages of Clifford Geertz's "Deep Play: Notes on a Balinese Cockfight"—the second of his essays I met as an undergraduate—beautifully illustrate the movement between summary and scene. The essay begins with a summary of the writer's arrival in Bali:

> Early in April of 1958, my wife and I arrived, malarial and diffident, in a Balinese village we intended, as anthropologists, to study. A small place, about five hundred people, and relatively remote, it was its own world. We were intruders, professional ones, and the villagers dealt with us as Balinese seem always to deal with people not part of their life who yet press themselves upon them: as though we were not there. For them, and to a degree for ourselves, we were nonpersons, specters, invisible men.

The next two pages continue orienting the reader to an unfamiliar setting, as the Geertzes settle in, yet remain nonpersons. Then, some ten days after their arrival, they learn about a cockfight that will be held in a public square. Geertz adds more background, explaining that cockfights are illegal in Bali and thus are usually held in secluded spaces. He then switches to a scene now embedded in the imaginations of most cultural anthropologists:

> In the midst of the third match, with hundreds of people, including, still transparent, myself and my wife, fused into a single body around the ring, a superorganism in the literal sense, a truck full of policemen armed with machine guns roared up. Amid great screeching cries of "pulisi! pulisi!" from the crowd, the policemen jumped out, and springing into the center of the ring, began to swing their guns around like gangsters in a motion picture, though not going so far as actually to fire them. The superorganism came instantly apart as its components scattered in all directions. People raced down the road, disappeared headfirst over walls, scrambled under platforms, folded themselves behind wicker screens, scuttled up coconut trees. Cocks armed with steel spurs sharp enough to cut off a finger or run a hole through a foot were running wildly around. Everything was dust and panic.

After establishing this chaotic scene, Geertz places himself and his wife, Hildred, inside the action. They join the running crowd, even though it is headed away from where they live. Just as the rice fields open out, offering no cover, the man ahead of them turns into a compound, and they follow. The man's wife immediately sets up a table and serves tea. When the police arrive, the Geertzes primly play along with their host's insistence that they had been drinking tea and knew nothing of a cockfight.

From this scene, the narrative gathers the momentum of summary, jumping to the next day, when the anthropologists find themselves greeted by villagers who beg to hear endless repetitions of their account. Geertz then pulls back to an even wider-angle generalizing summary: "In Bali, to be teased is to be accepted . . ." He proceeds to describe how finally he had achieved rapport. As he moves into his summary account of cockfighting as a cultural practice, images from the dramatic event remain vividly present.

Geertz's scene represents a turning point for fieldwork. "Turning points" is also the first category of scenes with dramatic potential that

Theodor Rees Cheney advises creative nonfiction writers to look for. Here is his suggestive list:

turning points	*showdowns*	*arguments*
flashbacks	*disasters*	*hardships*
successes	*failures*	*life reversals*
beginnings	*births*	*deaths*

To identify such scenes is to begin assembling the building blocks of a story.

▹ Write a scene related to any one of Cheney's categories. Start with the prompt "A turning point [or showdown, argument, flashback, etc.] that I particularly want to tell you about is . . ." (10 minutes to start a sketch that you can refine and add to later)

Now that you have started writing this scene, I will suggest two different ways to revise and extend your piece. First, pause to reflect on the style of telling that you chose: what perspective, which tone? Raymond Queneau's *Exercises in Style* offers a playful example of how the same scene can be retold in many different ways. Queneau was a French novelist, publisher, philosopher, and mathematician. In short takes, each a page or two long, his book tells and retells two encounters with a stranger distinguished by a long neck and funny hat: once on a Paris bus and once, later the same day, near a train station. Queneau's English translator, Barbara Wright, quotes him as telling an interviewer, "I started from a real incident, and in the first place I told it 12 times in different ways. Then a year later I did another 12, and finally there were 99." Queneau clearly had great fun spoofing the peculiarities of different prose genres, voices, points of views, rhetorical tropes, and more. Looking through even a few of these exercises is a reminder of the sprawling multiplicity of forms in which we might choose to write. As the sociologist Howard Becker shows in his book *Telling about Society*, there are many different ways in which specialists (like ethnographers), artists, and laypeople take on the task of describing social life. Though you may be writing within a particular form, through your choice or disciplinary constraints, briefly allow yourself to play, at least briefly, with the possibility of retelling your scene in an entirely different way.

▹ Consider the different media, beyond written form, that you might use to represent the scene you chose. Then return to words

and consider the different ways that a scene could be communicated. Begin writing about the same scene from the vantage of a different narrator, or a different genre—for example, as a poem, song, play, personal essay, or short story. (10 minutes for this experiment that might start you off on an unforeseen journey)

Second, read over the scene you originally began writing. Consider what a reader would need to know to understand what lies within and behind the details you've evoked. What aspects of a larger backdrop might you need to summarize?

For cultural analysts, the move between scenes and summaries might also be conceived of in terms of events and contexts. But contexts are neither preordained nor neutral: events gain particular meaning through the aspects of context we choose to highlight. Geertz describes police disrupting a cockfight to illustrate the building of rapport and to introduce readers to the importance of cockfighting as a Balinese form of cultural interpretation. Yet this event would acquire different meanings if he had more fully placed the arriving police and the scattering crowd in relation to state violence in Indonesia in the early 1960s.

The contexts that serve as backdrops to events can include larger historical processes. So for example, another influential anthropologist, Sally Falk Moore, argues that ethnography should show "how local events and local commentary on them can be linked to a variety of processes unfolding simultaneously on very different scales of time and place." She makes a helpful distinction between "foreground preoccupations," or what people themselves make of events, and "background conditions" that surround and inform these events.

▹ Revisit your written scene and begin a list of what you would consider to be the "foreground preoccupations" of the people you describe, and the "background conditions" of larger unfolding processes. (5 minutes)

Situation, Story, Theory

Both creative nonfiction and ethnography mix stories and ideas, but creative nonfiction often highlights the storytelling, while conventional academic ethnography more closely follows disciplinary conventions for citation and argument, with more emphasis on engaging ideas and less on an engaging story. Between these two paths, of course, is a vast realm of possibilities.

What makes a good story? Obviously, this is a matter of taste (both personal and cultural), but I usually think in terms of intriguing characters and shifts in awareness or in power relations. Contradictions and conflicts push change, from within or without. A story doesn't need to be told chronologically, or in complete detail; what's omitted, or withheld for a time, may be as significant as what's included. You can select key scenes and play with their order: written time can move backward or sideways or advance in leaps. You can build suspense by not giving away the story's journey or destination in advance.

I learned a useful distinction between situation and story from the memoirist Vivian Gornick. As she puts it, "The situation is the context or circumstance, sometimes the plot; the story is the emotional experience that preoccupies the writer: the insight, the wisdom, the thing one has come to say." Adapting this distinction for ethnographers, the *situation* might include the site of fieldwork, various personal circumstances, the historical and social moment, and even prevailing theories about the subject of research. The *story*, though, follows the transformations—physical, emotional, intellectual—that an ethnographer experiences personally or witnesses in others.

In his manifesto on fieldwork and ethnography that opens *Argonauts of the Western Pacific*, Bronislaw Malinowski instructs readers: "Imagine yourself suddenly set down surrounded by all your gear alone on a tropical beach close to a native village while the launch or dinghy which has brought you sails away out of sight." Embarking on that thick book in graduate school, I saw the waves crashing, coconut palms waving, the outlines of a village nearby, and the boat sailing away through a glare of sea and sky. By presenting himself in an interesting situation as a field researcher, Malinowki was beckoning readers forward with the possibility of an unusual story. Many widely read ethnographies similarly play up the storytelling potential of landing in a radically unfamiliar situation.

When I separate story and situation, I think also of what my friend Rasha said when she read an early draft of the manuscript that became my family memoir, *My Family and Other Saints*. Rasha and I had grown up together, and I knew her perspective would enrich mine. She is now a product designer, and I hadn't anticipated the gift of her designer's eye. "It seems to me that now you've laid out all the materials," she said, "but you still have to decide on the *design*. Then you'll know which materials you'll use and which you don't really need." I suddenly saw how the first half of the manuscript was unnecessary; background information that I could summarize. The story I really wanted to tell was lodged in the second half, which followed the spiritual quests that my older brother embarked on and that came to affect the whole family. I started afresh with a sleeker narrative design, beginning the story this time from what had been the midpoint, and expanding from there.

Here is an exercise to help identify some of the story or stories carried within the situation that your material presents:

▹ Summarize the situation that you want to write about with a line each about time, place, personal circumstances, and the larger quest that informs this situation. List dramatic changes that emerged in any of these categories, as a way to begin identifying the tallest redwoods of story rising from that ground of experience. (15 minutes)

Don't be alarmed if you feel lost in the woods and at first can't figure out what the main story might be. Stories often grow in groves, with some stunted by the shadows of others. Like enormous trees disappearing into the sky, big and emotionally compelling stories tend to point beyond what we can immediately see. Sometimes you may need to move through more than one complete draft before you sense the story or stories with the broadest span and the greatest import for a particular project.

Notice whether the stories you've chosen are more about your own experience or the experiences of others. The stories that others share, as ethnographers know, are an invaluable resource to learn from and to write with. Malinowski famously exhorted ethnographers to find "the native's point of view." Most readers citing that passage stop there. But it's worth remembering the lines that come after: "We have to study man, and we must study what concerns him most intimately, that is, the hold which life has on him." We need to know, he writes, "the subjective desire of feeling by what these people live . . . realizing the substance of their happiness." This means stretching beyond oneself to try and fathom what the world looks like from other perspectives—a compassionate challenge in any situation and all the more complicated when dealing with people unlike oneself, whether they live far away or close by. Coexisting with others through time increases the chance of being able to grasp their points of view, their feelings, their stories. To engage with these everyday stories—and to translate that engagement into what Lila Abu-Lughod has called "ethnographies of the particular"—is to move beyond cultural generalizations and potentially challenge prevailing theories.

What do others say about their own stories? What do you discern? Conventional markers like "once upon a time"; the themes that the story addresses; and the situations in which stories are habitually told all reveal the sort of story it could be.

▹ What kinds of stories have you assembled from others? Write a line each on the their form (recognizable shape), themes (subject matter), and contexts (occasions for telling). (10 minutes)

From my own research on oral narrative, I know that the exercise I've suggested can be expanded into book-length projects, especially if you include the full texts of stories themselves. Your choice of stories will be connected to the larger theme you're exploring. Swamiji, an old Hindu holy man central to my dissertation and first book, connected story to situation in a particular way:

> When you tell a story, you should look at the situation and tell it. Then it turns out well. If you just tell any story any time, it's not really good. You must consider the time and shape the story so it's right. All stories are told for some purpose.

What is your purpose in choosing a particular story? You might decide to *show* insights through the story rather than state what these are. You might want to express your reasons for reproducing or retelling certain stories in everyday, nontheoretical language. Here it's very helpful to start with what the people you're trying to describe might say about the concepts you are writing about. How does their perspective diverge from the ways that specialists might debate these issues? (Chekhov's character Misail, for example, noted that the laborers for whom work was "obligatory and inevitable" didn't seem to debate "the moral significance of labor," or even to use the word "labor" in their conversations.)

As the anthropologist Marilyn Strathern points out, for ethnographers, "The question is not simply how to bring certain scenes to life but how to bring life to ideas." These ideas guiding your work draw on prior conversations. If you are working with the more specialized language of theory to build an explicit argument, I will assume that you have already identified the conceptual categories directing your choice of particular scenes, summaries, situations, or stories. Otherwise, consider authors working in a similar terrain.

▹ Sketch out, as conversations, the viewpoints of a few key authors whose work sheds light on yours in terms of, first, the geographical area and, second, the theoretical terrain. Characterize the tone and dramatic turning points in both exchanges. (15 minutes)

Can you locate an opening in these conversations where you might join in with a "Yes, and . . ." or "But what my materials show that . . ." or "If you look at it this way . . ." or "Have you noticed that . . . ?" What new insight or revealing perspective does your work bring to these discussions?

▹ Return to the authors with whom you share theoretical terrain, this time not naming them but instead naming the central concepts they address. Freewrite a few lines about how you hope to join the conversations and revise the concepts, beginning, "I argue that . . ." (10 minutes)

Chekhov as Ethnographic Muse

A few pages photocopied from Chekhov's *Sakhalin Island* appeared in my campus mailbox in early 2009, hidden amid the usual chaos of interdepartmental envelopes, publishers' catalogs, and announcements of university events. I was teaching a graduate seminar on ethnographic writing, and my friend and colleague Frank Salomon had left me these pages. I didn't read the extracts immediately, but once I did, I wanted to find the entire book; once I looked at the book, I became curious about Chekhov's larger work and life. I was already working on this manuscript, but the promise and pleasure of discovery began to transform my plans for one chapter after another.

I may never be able to fully articulate the reasons that Chekhov took such a powerful hold on my imagination, but I see at least three ways that he might provide inspiration to authors of ethnographic or ethnographically informed writing. First, he demonstrates an ethnographer's ability to move between social locations: his writing draws on a stunning range of social perspectives, places, and lifeworlds. Second, he shows by example how professional identities can coexist, bringing energy to creative aspirations: his life as a doctor and a writer in many genres holds out hope for anyone who writes both as a scholar and in other voices, or who moves between ethnographic insight and social activism. Third, partly because of his shifting social perspectives and fluid movement between writing genres, Chekhov was pointedly, even hilariously, articulate on problems of representation. I'll weave these three points through a quick account of his life (which overlaps, in scattered details, with that of his character Misail in "My Life").

Anton Pavlovitch Chekhov—"Antosha" to family and friends—was born in 1860 in the multiethnic town of Taganrog, a port on the Sea of Azov, a northern arm of the Black Sea. His parents were both children of serfs who had bought their own freedom, and so he had direct ties to peasant life. When Chekhov was sixteen, his father, a shopkeeper, declared bankruptcy and took off for Moscow; the rest of the family followed him to that distant city while Chekhov stayed on in the ruins of his former life, finishing school. He managed to gain a scholarship to study medicine in Moscow, where he joined his family and began his transformation from "provincial boy" to "urban cosmopolitan intellectual." While his scholarship stipend helped support his parents and siblings, as a nineteen-year-old he began augmenting this income by writing short comic pieces for magazines and journals—sketches, cartoon captions, reviews, stories, and whatever else he could sell. His work as a doctor brought him close knowledge of patients from a wide range of backgrounds, and as his literary standing grew, he interacted with admirers from many strata of society and corners of Russia.

Perhaps this access to vastly different social locations and perspectives contributed to Chekhov's wariness of fixed labels. He engaged with life as both participant and observer, viewing what others took for granted from a skeptical, questioning remove. Critics who sought to define him were frustrated by his resistance to any single intellectual or political position. At first he wrote under a variety of pen names, especially "Antosha Chekhonte," reserving his real name for his future professional identity as a doctor. At twenty-six, when his first collection of stories was being published, he wavered until the last minute about whether Antosha Chekhonte would be the author; Anton Chekhov won out. But even as Anton Chekhov grew in stature, writing longer, more serious stories and plays, Antosha Chekhonte's droll voice and delight in absurd detail continued to surface like a light fizz in a strong drink. At twenty-eight, when he was finding recognition as a writer, Chekhov complained of others' desire to pin him down. Writing to the older editor and poet A. N. Pleshcheyev (who, along with Dostoevsky, had been imprisoned for participation in a progressive literary circle and had ended up spending ten years in Siberia), Chekhov spelled out some of his core beliefs:

> I look upon labels and tags as prejudices. My holy of holies is the human body, health, intelligence, talent, inspiration, love, and the most absolute freedom imaginable, freedom from violence and lies, no matter what form the latter two take. Such is the program I would adhere to if I were a major artist.
>
> But I've gone on too much as it is. Keep well.
>
> Yours,
> A. Chekhov

The modesty of the hypothetical "if I were a major artist" and the self-effacing awareness of perhaps being long-winded are among the reasons I find Chekhov not just admirable but endearing.

Chekhov often joked about the multiple tugs on his time and creative energy. When his patron and for many years principal correspondent, the newspaper editor Alexei Suvorin, chided him about "chasing two hares" as a doctor and writer, Chekhov responded that he saw nothing wrong with this:

> I feel more alert and more satisfied with myself when I think of myself as having two occupations instead of one. Medicine is my lawful wedded wife, and literature my mistress. When one gets on my nerves, I spend the night with the other. This may be somewhat disorganized, but then again it's not as boring, and anyway, neither one loses anything by my duplicity. If I didn't have medicine, I'd never devote my spare time and thoughts to literature. I lack discipline.

Fiction and playwriting also competed: "The narrative form is a lawful wife, whereas the dramatic form is a gaudy, loud-mouthed, brazen and tiresome mistress." And his one nonfiction work further complicated the ménage: "I'm working on my Sakhalin book and, in between times, so as not to starve my family to death, I caress my muse and write short stories." Reading these lines, I was entertained but also a little judgmental—just how might these metaphors reflect the handsome charmer's attitudes toward women? But in Chekhov's time, as my mother wearily reminded me, hadn't marriage represented respectable social responsibility, while a mistress meant following one's passions? Looking across the span of his life, Chekhov seems to have balanced his roles as "husband" and "lover," maintaining identities both as doctor and as writer in many genres, and eventually marrying a woman with whom he'd long enjoyed a passionate affair.

Chekhov also combined his literary and medical identities with social engagement. Even when he no longer primarily relied on medicine for a living, he continued to practice as a doctor, treating family and friends, as well as peasants, at no charge. He took on the arduous journey across Siberia to witness conditions in the Sakhalin prison settlement in 1890, helped organize famine relief in the winter of 1891, and worked with fellow doctors in battling the cholera epidemic that followed in 1892. In addition, he established several schools for peasants, helped out with a census, and built up public libraries with big shipments of books. While constantly acting in these politically informed ways, he did not always speak out politically. But in 1898, when the rigged case against the Jewish army officer Alfred Dreyfus was reopened by French courts and the writer Émile Zola (who had defended Dreyfus's innocence, pointing to a conspiracy) was tried for libel, Chekhov, then visiting Nice, was outraged. He studied the transcripts of the original trial to add force to his support of Dreyfus and Zola. He argued fiercely against the anti-Semitic tone in Russian newspaper coverage, and especially the newspaper owned by Suvorin, his patron and, until this time, his close friend. Chekhov took another public stand a few years later, resigning from the Russian Academy of Sciences in protest after the writer Maxim Gorky was excluded because of his political opinions.

Even with his literary success, Chekhov was often strapped for funds. This was at least partly because he was always helping others out with gifts and loans: not just his immediate family, but friends and also strangers who appealed to him. (In his will, he instructed that after his immediate relatives died, his estate be used to support public education in his birthplace, Taganrog.) Many of the people he helped in his lifetime wrote letters of gratitude, and during the Soviet era over seven thousand of these extant letters to Chekhov were compiled by the "Socio-Economic Publishing House." Since it wasn't always clear what people were grateful for, the publisher added explanatory notes such as—and here I am not inventing—"Chekhov lent Kirin money for a trip to Kolomna"!

Chekhov has lent me his words—and more. As I've composed this short portrait, I've been reminded of a letter he wrote to a friend from Nice in the spring of 1898, when he was already a famous writer and playwright, worthy of an oil portrait:

> Braz is painting my portrait. At the studio. I sit in an armchair which has a green velvet back. *En face*. White tie. People say that both the tie and I are a good likeness, but my expression, as last year, looks as if I'd taken a great whiff of horseradish . . .

Writing about Chekhov, I've often wondered if I've got both the likeness and the expression right. Again and again, as I've tried to recall a quip, I've ended up mangling the word order, reminding me how, even in translation, his precision with language gleams like a doctor's instruments. I've sprinkled some of Chekhov's observations on writing through this book as they apply to nonfiction rather than fiction; for a fuller scope of his thoughts on writing, I highly recommend Piero Brunello and Lena Lenček's compilation *How to Write Like Chekhov* (2008).

Chekhov often found himself criticized for remaining vague about what he thought readers should learn from his stories—that is, he held back from drawing explicit conclusions or spelling out underlying convictions. In another of his many letters to Suvorin, Chekhov defended himself by drawing a distinction between "*solving a question* and *posing a question correctly*." Specialists might focus on solving questions, while artists pose them: "An artist observes, selects, conjectures, arranges—and these very acts presuppose as their starting point a question—for if from the start he's not set himself a question, there would be nothing to conjecture or select."

Notice, though, that Chekhov doesn't foreclose the possibility of a text both posing a question through representation, and embarking on an answer through analysis. Indeed, *Sakhalin Island* attempts to do both. Questioning the social inequalities, capitalist rapaciousness, industrial growth, repressive state policies, and environmental destruction of his times—and also the complexities of human hearts—Chekhov came up with new forms for stories, plays, and nonfiction. As he wrote in the notebook that was his storehouse of odds and ends to be worked into future projects: "New literary forms always produce new forms of life and that is why they are so revolting to the conservative human mind."

Even before Chekhov was officially diagnosed with tuberculosis in his late thirties, he had struggled with periodic bouts of coughing, spitting blood, low energy, and a variety of other ailments. Perhaps these challenges to his health contributed to his dispassionate sense of life itself as something marvelous and strange. Toward the end of "My Life," Marya Viktorovna is setting off to the Chicago World's Fair and writes Misail to report that she's ordered herself a ring inscribed "Everything passes." Misail reflects that if he were to order such a ring it would instead read "Nothing passes." As he says, "I believe that nothing passes without a trace and that each of our smallest steps has significance for the present and the future." Or in "The Story of the Unknown Man," the upper-class spy who has posed as a house servant and who is suffering from tuberculosis says, "Life is given only once, and one would like to live it cheerfully, meaningfully, beautifully . . ." Maxim Gorky recalled Chekhov lying on a sofa, playing with a thermometer, and saying between coughs, "To live simply to die is by no means amusing, but to live with the knowledge that you will die before your time, that really is idiotic." Chekhov died of complications from tuberculosis when he was only forty-four.

I look back on the many months that I have felt driven to learn more about Chekhov and how, unexpectedly, this helped me write the book you now hold. Earlier, I suggested a prompt about the central insights you'd like your work to carry. I end this chapter with a more open-ended invitation to honor the force of your own curiosity. Whether your work is driven more by story or by argument, whether you are writing within an established genre or venturing into a new form, *consider the questions* that motivate you as you select, conjecture about, and arrange your observations. Try this exercise as a way of spelling out your curiosity for yourself:

▹ Start with "I am most curious about . . ." and write forward. (2 minutes)

As you move forward with the exercises ahead, and especially when you're flagging, I suggest periodically returning to the wellspring of your own curiosity. When what you're writing about starts to seem so obvious that you can't motivate yourself to continue, remind yourself of why you were once curious and try to communicate that to yourself as much as to a possible reader.

* · *

STORY AND THEORY

Begin narrating an event that dramatizes the central idea or issue you want to write about. Drawing on all of your senses, use vivid details to describe the people and the place as you follow what happened. For now, don't explicitly say what concept you're trying to illuminate; only show life in process. 2 pages.

THEORY AND STORY

Now step back and identify the larger guiding ideas you have brought to this situation and that alerted you to the event as worth recording. If you are drawing on specialist language, try to translate into terms intelligible to the uninitiated. Explain the logic of the ideas—citing predecessors as needed—and then summarize the event as an example. 2 pages.

TWO Place

Two months after he arrived by ship at the tsarist prison colony on Sakhalin, thirty-year-old Anton Chekhov again boarded the *Baikal* to sail from the north to the south of the island. For years he had managed to write amid a hubbub of sociability. While the captain, officers, and a few jolly fellow passengers chatted and laughed below deck, Chekhov composed a letter to his friend Suvorin. "I saw everything," he reported, "so the problem now is not *what* I saw, but *how* I saw it":

> I don't know what I'll end up with, but I've gotten a good deal accomplished. I have enough for three dissertations. I got up every day at five in the morning, went to bed late, and spent all my days worrying about how much I had yet to do. Now that I'm done with the penal colony, I have the feeling I've seen it all, but missed the elephant.

Ethnographers will recognize Chekhov's dilemma: midstream in a project, not knowing what form the materials you are gathering will take, you can't be sure you've done enough. No matter how hard you've worked, what might you have missed? In your painstaking focus on recording concrete details, have you overlooked larger patterns? Chekhov was apparently alluding to a fable by the Russian writer Ivan Krylov: a man visits a natural history museum and is so entranced by a display of tiny insects that he doesn't notice the huge stuffed elephant.

But why was Chekhov thinking of his materials in terms of dissertations?

After receiving his medical degree in 1884, Chekhov had immediately begun practicing as a doctor. He had also continued publishing short stories, and in 1888 his third collection of stories won half of the prestigious Pushkin literary prize. With such success, why bother about a dissertation? But the idea of a medical dissertation had been on his mind for years; proving himself in this way would earn him the credentials required to lecture at Moscow University. The topic of the prison settlement was actually his third idea; he had earlier considered writing a history of gender inequality or a history of the practice of medicine in Russia.

For at least two centuries the tsarist government had been deporting prisoners east to the Siberian expanses. The island of Sakhalin, off the Pacific coast, was a relatively recent acquisition: Russians had claimed the northern part since 1857, but only after 1875 was the southern section ceded to Russia by Japan. Since then, the government had been actively colonizing the island, shipping in large numbers of convicts for both labor and settlement. Chekhov had become interested in Sakhalin in the fall of 1889, when he happened to read some lecture notes on criminal law and prison management that his younger brother Mikhail was reviewing for civil service exams.

Chekhov's family and friends were bewildered when he announced his intention to take on the difficult three-month trip across Siberia to Sakhalin—the furthest one could travel from Moscow within the multiethnic Russian empire. He confused everyone (including his eventual biographers) by tossing around assorted reasons for his journey, and the timing of his travels suggests yet more possibilities. He may have been despondent after his older brother's death from tuberculosis, restless after his enormous literary success, eager to respond to critics who attacked him for a lack of explicit social conscience, stung by the poor reception of his play *The Wood Demon*, fleeing from further entanglement with his sister's gray-eyed friend Lika Mizinova. In the spring of 1890, when his friend and editor Suvorin tried to dissuade him from going, telling him that nobody was interested in Sakhalin, Chekhov mentioned both his recently neglected medical career and his social conscience. He wrote Suvorin that he wanted to "write at least one or two hundred pages to pay off some of my debt to medicine, toward which, as you know, I've behaved like a pig." He also sharply countered his more conservative friend's claim that no one was interested in the prison settlement. People should be interested in "a place of unbearable suffering," Chekhov insisted; by not showing interest, other citizens—not just prison wardens—became morally culpable.

Through that spring, Chekhov prepared himself for research in Sakhalin by methodically reading and taking notes on everything he could find that had been written about the island and the Russian prison system—including articles on Siberia by the American journalist George Keenan, whose work was officially banned in Russia. (His ever-supportive younger sister Masha and her friends helped out with this background research.) "I spend all day reading and taking notes," Chekhov reported to another friend. "In my head and on paper there's nothing but Sakhalin. It's a kind of madness. *Mania Sachalinosa.*"

Steeping oneself in prior writing about a place is of course familiar to ethnographers. But while ethnographers have usually gone on to spend at least a year in the field, Chekhov spent only three months in Sakhalin—the brief summer season. He arrived in the northern part of the island in July, sailed to the south in September, and started on his journey home in October, traveling by ship through Hong Kong and Singapore toward Ceylon, and then on to Odessa.

In those three months, Chekhov gathered an astonishing amount of material. He produced statistics on each settlement. He printed up ten thousand cards for a makeshift census of the men, women, and children to whom he was allowed access (he was officially forbidden to speak to political prisoners). He spoke to prisoners who lived in cells and were let out, chains clinking, for hard labor; to laboring prisoners who were allowed to live outside the prisons with their families; and to "freed settlers" who had served out their sentences but were required to remain on the island. These conversations revealed facts, attitudes, and life stories. Chekhov also observed and spoke to the many Russian bureaucrats who oversaw these operations. And he briefly interacted with indigenous Gilyak and Ainu people whose ways of life were being brutally transformed by colonization.

"Travel notes" is how Chekhov first subtitled the work he eventually produced, but with his scientifically oriented medical background and his literary skills, he had ventured far beyond a travel book; he wrote *Sakhalin Island* partly as a scholarly contribution and partly as a way to alert general readers to the appalling conditions on Sakhalin (all while facing the challenge of navigating the book past the tsarist censor). Though he never called *Sakhalin Island* an ethnography, I discern many ethnographic aspects in its pages: in Chekhov's pointed awareness of how people's lives are shaped by larger systems; in his ear for different ways of speaking and all that is conveyed beyond content; in his eye for vivid and telling details. *Sakhalin Island* is a long and cumbrous book. For anyone who would like a sense of its flashes of brilliance, and its contemporary relevance to creative nonfiction and ethnography alike, the translators Piero Brunello and Lena Lenček have included short passages in their compilation *How to Write Like Chekhov*. As I consider different approaches to ethnographically representing a place, I too draw on *Sakhalin Island*, interweaving short sections with selections from other ethnographers' work.

When ethnography was first established as a way of researching and writing about other people's lives, "the field" as a site of research for anthropologists referred to a culturally different and out-of-the-way, bounded place. As ideas of which places might appropriately be considered the field have shifted, so too have techniques for fieldwork and modes of representation. Ethnographers now find the field in the familiar and the metropolitan, in archives, markets, corporations, laboratories, media worlds, cyberspaces, and more. Moreover, as places are more complexly connected to other places through the intensifying forces of globalization, the field can stretch across networks of sites. For the exercises that follow, the place you're writing about could be distant or nearby, conceptually demarcated or far-flung. You might be drawing from your own notes and memories, or from accounts produced by others.

The Scene of Writing

Most writing about place involves more than one kind of place: the place being described, certainly, but also the physical site of the writing. A good way to limber up and simply start writing about place is to observe what's around you at the very moment that you're writing. For example, trying to write a first draft of this chapter, unable to find my voice or to figure out a way to arrange notes, I forced myself to look around and start finding words for the place I sat:

> All peaking angles and shades of white, the walls of the loft are gauzy with summer afternoon heat. The blossoming linden tree's greens and yellows refract through the low arched window to the south. The sky shimmers through the windows to the north and east. Shades are pulled closed on the other skylights. As I look around, seated at the desk, the air conditioner at my right valiantly labors to cool the room; above me, the overhead fan spins. The heat finally evicts me and I reestablish contact with this paragraph downstairs on a laptop. Already, the place I was trying to describe through direct observation is moving toward a description from remembered images and the rearranging of words.

You probably aren't that interested in this loft or the linden tree outside my window, but they show up often, season after season, in the journal that I try to write in every morning. The tree, along with the pale apricot light traced by morning sun, rainbows scattered from a prism, and the companionable presence of cats basking in upper-story warmth, invariably rescues me from sluggish silence. I find that placing myself at the moment of writing grounds a skittishly distracted mind, bringing the present into better focus and so adding clarity to other ventures too. Try this:

▹ **Write a few lines about where you are as you're trying to write.**

You might never reread this description or share it with other readers. Or you might be taking notes about a place that you hope to write about in the future, in which case this could become material you will later mine. Whatever the outcome, becoming present to observe what's around you should help you get started with threading connections between perceptions and words. I find this practice a reminder that all life is worth honoring with attention, not just what's been delineated as a Project. (I have also used this prompt in classes, giving everyone five minutes to describe the classroom; everyone seems entertained to learn how others see a familiar space, and comparing writings invariably starts a discussion on representation.)

Writing what's around you, you'll immediately notice how much you leave out. Many details fall out in a quick sketch, as they should, since the representation is made from the perspective of a particular moment, and so conveys a particular preoccupation and mood. Too many painstakingly elaborated details can overwhelm a reader and end up accomplishing less than the bold strokes of an immediate sensory impression. A friend who teaches nonfiction writing once told me about an exercise she uses in her class: the students first describe a place from memory and then, later, go to the place and describe it, the first description invariably has more life and energy, she said, while the second is deadened by a piling on of conscientious detail.

Look again at what you've written. Are the details primarily visual? All too often, vision predominates in ethnographic descriptions. Consciously drawing on the full range of senses can evoke a place more thoroughly. Return again to where you are writing.

▹ Make a list engaging all five senses, if possible. Be as specific and precise as you can: an image, a smell, a sound, a taste, a texture or touch.

Passage to More Than a Place

We all carry around bundles of associations and assumptions about places. Many of these have been handed over, unexamined, from other sources. Try unpacking your own associations, contemplate where you picked them up, and consider whether they evaporate under close scrutiny or condense some real-life insight. This will help you locate your own writing and will also help you grasp what your readers may be expecting.

When I first arrived in the United States as a sixteen-year-old, I was often perplexed by people's reactions when I told them where I'd grown up. "India!" some exclaimed with shining eyes. "Yes, India . . . ," others pronounced with concern. Yet others smiled meaningfully: "Aah, IN-dia . . ." In each case, I had to guess what associations might have provoked their reactions. Years later, in graduate school, I discovered an essay by Milton Singer, the Chicago-based anthropologist of India, that helped me place some of these responses within centuries of Western encounter with India. In his cleverly titled essay "Passage to More Than India," Singer describes the historical underpinnings of diverse images: the opulent, marvelous India of maharajas, gold, brocades, and spices; the problem-ridden India of poverty, disease, caste subjugation, and oppressed women; the spiritual India of ancient texts, nonviolent resistance, gurus, meditation, and yoga. As Singer points out, images generated by outsiders can be folded into self-images. Many more images of India have emerged in the decades since his essay was written—for example those associated with communal violence, nuclear power, Bollywood extravaganzas, call centers, booming economic growth—but the earlier images also remain in brisk circulation.

▹ **List a few images popularly associated with the place you want to write about (for example, categories of people, kinds of objects, activities, colors, smells, tastes).**

Place-names can also reveal complex transcultural histories. “India,” for example, recalls Persian and Arabic references to “Hind” or “al-Hind” as the land beyond the Indus (Sindhu), and also ancient Greek accounts of “Indika.”

“Sakhalin,” Chekhov learned, derived from a French misreading of a map commissioned by the Chinese emperor in the early eighteenth century that in turn drew on charts made by Japanese seafarers. This Chinese map carried an inscription *Saghalien-Angahata* (in Mongolian, “Cliffs of the Black River”), indicating an area near the mouth of the Amur River on the mainland west of the island. In France, though, this inscription was mistaken for the name of the island, and this is how it came to be known on European maps.

Chekhov’s attention to names continued through his travels. With understated irony, he observed that it was “interesting”—some translations read “curious”—how settlements in Sakhalin were named by Russian colonizers to honor “governors of Siberia, prison governors and even doctors’ assistants” rather than important early explorers. Authorities had named these settlements; streets, though, he found were sometimes named by or after settlers themselves. So for example, the settlement of Rykovskoye or Rykovo, named after a prison governor called Rykov, contained a “Sizovskaya Street, so called because the cabin of the female settled exile Sizovskaya stands on the corner.”

▹ **List a few names of places important to your project. How might these names reveal power relations? What cultural values do you perceive through them?**

In *Wisdom Sits in Places*, Keith Basso describes how members of the White Mountain Apache tribe in Arizona use place-names and stories about places as moral teachings: a place-name like "Shades of Shit" encapsulates a story about selfish people who wouldn't share their corn and sickened, while "Line of White Rocks Extends Up and Out" evokes a girl who disregarded her grandmother's counsel. At various times, these stories might be alluded to by just pronouncing the name of the place; or they might be summarized in an outline; or they might be retold at length, with narrative flair. In all these cases, the story's work is reinforced by its ongoing presence in the landscape.

▹ **Reflect on how place-names associated with your project convey shared stories. Choose a name and retell what you know about the story behind it.**

The Feel of a Place

Reading transports us. How do ethnographers enhance this journey so that readers glean facts about a place and also something of the feel of being there? Describing one region of Sakhalin, Chekhov begins with statistics: "There are, on average, 189 days with precipitation in a year: 107 with snow and 82 with rain." He goes on to describe the many weeks "with clouds the colour of lead" and their depressive effect on inhabitants. But before the end of the paragraph, he situates these numbers and generalities about wet, dank weather through an observed moment: "Once on a clear sunlit day, I saw a wall of perfectly white, milk-coloured mist pour in from the sea; it was as if a white curtain had been lowered from the sky to earth."

Here is how Margaret Mead describes the crushing midday heat in her chapter "A Day in Samoa," which sets the stage for *Coming of Age in Samoa*:

> It is high noon. The sun burns the feet of the little children, who leave their palm leaf balls and their pin-wheels of frangipani blossoms to wither in the sun, as they creep into the shade of the houses. The women who must go abroad carry great banana leaves as sunshades or wind wet cloths about their heads. Lowering a few blinds against the slanting sun, all who are left in the village wrap their heads in sheets and go to sleep. Only a few adventurous children may slip away for a swim in the shadow of a high rock, some industrious woman continue with her weaving, or a close little group of women bend anxiously over a woman in labour. The village is daz-

> zling and dead; any sound seems oddly loud and out of place. Words have to cut through the solid heat slowly.

Notice how Mead doesn't just settle for "terribly hot" but shows the heat pushing people indoors and into the shade; the practices of alleviating heat with banana leaves, wet cloths on the head, a cool swim; the standstill of regular village activity.

▹ **Describe a place at a particular time of day and the effects of this setting on social life.**

Moving from a tropical day, consider the far extreme: the cold in the Siberian taiga. In *The Reindeer People*, Piers Vitebsky follows the close association between the indigenous Eveny people and their reindeer in the wake of Soviet policies that transformed their nomadic ways of life. Going on a winter hunt with a retired herder, he mentions dressing in up to *fifteen layers* before venturing from the tent. Here is his entry from the first day of the hunt:

> The temperature today felt cold, but had not quite reached the threshold of −40 F. Below −40, the school would be closed and children sent home; helicopters and biplanes were not supposed to fly; saliva solidified before it hit the ground and if you threw hot tea up into the air, it froze and tinkled downward in a patter of little crystals.

The images of flash-frozen saliva and hot tea evoke the cold with a startling, visceral immediacy. Think of images that represent for you the power of heat, cold, moisture, smog, wind, waves, and other natural forces that shape people's lives.

▹ **Describe an image that encapsulates a powerful force in the environment, starting with "It was so ______ that . . ."**

You might also describe an entire season by running through a series of sensory impressions. In his book on Toba Batak wood carving in relation to tourism, Andrew Causey recreates the coming of the rainy season on Samosir Island in Lake Toba, Sumatra. He first evokes the sheer force and speed of a downpour through visual description:

> The gutter trench that surrounded my house and supposedly drained the water that fell on the small hill in my backyard puddled up white with mud water, then flowed translucent gray, then surged with water so quickly that it looked black.

Next, he turns to the shift in sounds, as the songbirds withdrew from the rain:

> Now, the thick, damp air was filled with the wheeze and croak of frogs in the newly formed pond or in the black trench water. Some nights, when the rain let up and became a sprinkle, their high-pitched croaking would drown out all other nighttime sounds so effectively that I could not tell if what I was hearing was a seamless amphibian chord surrounded by the vibrating sprinkle, or just ringing in my ear. If the drench of rain started up again, it only served to muffle their roar, not to obliterate it. Almost everyone in the village went to bed early on these drizzling nights because the sound of the TV could not be heard over the constant trilling of the frogs in the wet fields and ponds in the village.

Smells too became faint, washed away by the daily rain. Digging at the soil, Causey found that "far below the sensation of inhaling humidity, I caught a whiff of a very faint stink, something like a summer day's discovery that clothes had been left too long in the washer." The steady rains altered human routines as well: "The days were sullen, people kept their umbrellas close to the door, the families spent more time in the house together." With families staying in their homes and fewer tourists visiting, Causey found more opportunities to gain lively stories about tourist interactions from his local friends.

▹ **Describe a seasonal change as experienced through several senses, pointing to how it affected the landscape, people's everyday practices, and your project.**

Simile and metaphor can supplement concrete descriptive images to convey the feel of a place. The French anthropologist Jean Marie Gibbal researched the spirit cult of the Ghimbala river genii, who are attached to the northeast part of the Niger delta in Mali. In an early chapter of his book, he describes gliding along the River Niger in a long, black wooden pirogue with an arched hood, past areas diminished by drought and famine. Nearing the great expanse of water at Lake Debo, he observes how "the melancholy tuneful cries of the water birds, sea gulls among them, heighten the seaside feeling one gets in this place." Lake Debo, he writes, is a "little interior sea and a great reservoir of genie." Moving on from Lake Debo, past townships and sandbars,

> the Niger widens, narrows, strikes a difficult course across the Sahel's aridity, the earth increasingly denuded. The plain crouches under a sky veiled at times by light cirrus clouds like giant ripped sheets, whose filter turns the river's waters green. The walls at Danga, right on the river between Dire and Timbuktu, are painted with the hot colors of the setting sun. This evening we stop at the edge of a damp shallow that is vibrant with insects. Offshore, a band of hippopotamuses hold an all-night jubilee—complete with trumpeting, groans, and enormous smacks of sound—to the great displeasure of the local fisherpeople, who fear for their nets.

Take inspiration from Gibbal's use of metaphor, bridging disparate realms of experience: the *crouching* plain, *veiled* sky, *ripped sheets* of cloud, walls *painted* by sunset, the *jubilee* of large noisy animals, all contributing to the *seaside* feeling of the lake.

▹ Send your mind roaming toward other domains of your experience that could shed light on your description of a place. Begin with the prompt, "Being in ______ had the feel of . . ."

The literary critic Kenneth Burke has observed, "Every perspective requires a metaphor, implicit or explicit, for its organizational base." Ethnographers can gain descriptive depth by being alert not just to metaphors that enliven their own perception, but also the metaphors that the people living in a place regularly use.

Others' Perceptions

Jean Briggs shows how the Inuit people she lived with in the 1960s spoke of enjoying outdoor life through the seasons:

> Their eyes shine as they describe the thunder of the rapids in the spring and the might of the river when it lifts huge ice blocks and topples them, crashing, into itself. When the first ice forms in September, adults and children slide, laughing, on its black glass surface. "When winter comes you will learn to play," they told me—vigorous running games on the moonlit river. And the men, mending torn dog harnesses with long awkward stitches, sway heads and shoulders in imitation of a trotting dog, as they discuss a coming trip. Other men, whittling a winder fishing jig out of a bit of caribou antler, jerk it up and down tentatively in the hand, imitating the gesture

> of fishing, while humming a soft "ai ya ya," as they do while jigging, then laugh at themselves. "It's pleasant (*quvia*) to fish," they say. And in the spring, when the breeze loses its bite, there are endless hills of the sort "one wants to see the far side of."

With different times of year, then, people appreciate and interact with different aspects of the landscape.

▹ **Describe a place by enumerating a person's (or people's) descriptions of what they most look forward to through the seasons.**

Sometimes, people's perceptions may include animate and even deified forces in the environment. India's rivers, for example, are mostly seen by Hindus as goddesses to be propitiated, however polluted the waters may run. Julie Cruikshank has recorded how First Nations people of the Yukon perceive glaciers of the San Elias range to be sentient beings, "shape shifters of magnificent power." Her book *Do Glaciers Listen?* shows how Athapaskan and Tlingit stories about glaciers emphasize their humanlike characteristics:

> They respond to humans and especially to smells when meat is fried nearby. They are also quick to hear and to take offence when humans demonstrate cockiness by making jokes at their expense. They are apparently equipped with vision when, for example, they are characterized as giant worms "with eyes big as the moon."

Glaciers in these accounts are thought to sometimes show their own fierce agency as they observe and interact with humans. Cruikshank's book traces the great differences between such Yukon oral traditions, early travelers' journals, and more recent scientific accounts, showing how these competing views shape debates over land use in the area.

▹ **Describe an aspect of the place you are writing about (glaciers, rivers, hills, mountains, lakes, etc.) in terms of how its power and will are locally perceived.**

While Cruikshank, like Keith Basso, was instructed about the landscape through stories, in faraway Kalimantan, Indonesia, Anna Tsing was taught by her friend Ma Salam to "read the forest" for traces of human presence as she hiked in the early 1980s.

> It was with Ma Salam that I first learned how to walk though Meratus social space. Where I at first saw only the forest's natural beauty, he showed me how to read the forest socially. He taught me to dif-

> ferentiate the light green (*kuning*, also "yellow") leaves of secondary forest regrowing from old swiddens from the dark green (*hijau*, "green/blue") of the mature forest that begins slowly to show its presence after forty to fifty years of regrowth. He pointed to the remains of old cultivation and inhabitants that I might otherwise never have noticed. Red coleus leaves that once decorated the ritual "eye" (*pamataan*) of someone's rice field still flourished in five-year regrowth amid trees as thick as one's arm. Fruit pits once tossed out of someone's window had grown into productive trees before the forest was ten years old.

Notice how the colors, varieties, and ages of plants all reveal human action. Ken George, reading this chapter, also recalled how his friend Papa Ati took him out in the Sulawesi mountains for a lesson on how to listen to the sounds of spirit voices in the river.

▹ Describe someone showing you how they read or hear the landscape.

Know too that what you are writing becomes part of a historical document. All the places described in these quotations are likely to have changed since the ethnographers published their accounts.

Landscapes Transformed

Returning to Kalimantan a decade later, Anna Tsing found the same forests destroyed by logging and plantations. In her subsequent book *Friction* (2005), she describes walking along a logging road in the forested mountains of southeast Kalimantan:

> An abandoned logging road has got to be one of the most desolate places on earth. It doesn't go anywhere, by definition. If you are walking there, it is either because you are lost or you are trespassing, or both. The wet clay builds clods on your boots, if you have any, sapping your strength, and if you don't have any boots, the sun and the hot mud are unmerciful. Whole hillsides slide down beside you into the stagnant pools where the mosquitoes breed. Abandoned roads soon lose their shape, forcing you in and out of eroded canyons and over muddy trickles where bridges once stood but which are now choked by loose soil, vines crawling on disinterred roots and trunks sliding, askew. Yet, ironically, the forest as a site of truth and beauty seems much clearer from the logging road than anywhere else, since

> it is the road that slices open the neat cross-section in which underbrush, canopy, and high emergents are so carefully structured.

Notice how "you" becomes "me," the reader walking with Tsing and her Dayak companions as she induces in us the physical sensation, the discomfort and strain of slogging through the heavy, hot, wet clay and swarms of mosquitoes. At the same time, though, she opens our vision upward to the layered sweep of forest growth.

▹ Describe the emotional and bodily sensations of moving through a place.

Tsing moves on to describe how the old-growth forests rich in biodiversity have been leveled, replaced by "transmigration villages—Block A, Block B, Block C—and giant, miles-square plantations of oil palm, rubber, and acacia for the pulp and paper trade." Between the scrub and vines of cut stumps, the logging roads are worn arteries for looting resources from this new frontier. Her prior intimate knowledge of the forest adds to the sense of devastation as she chronicles the loss of trees, species, and ways of life, and the new social formations that have arisen. Bearing witness to environmental destruction is increasingly a painful aspect of ethnographic work and simply of living in these rapacious times.

Chekhov juxtaposes his observations of the banks of the River Duyka with a zoologist's description of the same river in 1881, just nine years earlier. Where the zoologist had recorded an enormous and ancient forest enfolding the river, and a marshy swampland, Chekhov found a river with banks so denuded that he was reminded of Moscow's city canal. The surrounding land too had been paved over, becoming the sprawling Alexandrovk settlement:

> Nowadays, in place of taiga, quagmires and ruts there stands a whole town, roads have been laid out, one sees the greenery of meadows, rye fields and vegetable gardens, and already complaints may be heard about the lack of forestry. If to this mass of toil and struggle, when they used to labour in the swamp up to the waist in water—if to this are added the frosts, the cold rains, yearning for their homeland, the insults, the birch rod—then appalling pictures arise in the imagination.

Into this description of a seemingly placid domesticated landscape, Chekhov has layered ecological devastation (a dedicated environmentalist, like some of the characters in his stories and plays, in his lifetime he planted scores of trees). He has also evoked the hardships of enforced convict labor that was the source of this transformation.

▹ Juxtapose a place as described at an earlier time (by yourself or another observer) and as you have more recently seen it. Bridging these two moments, what might you learn about people's labor and the power relations shaping the landscape?

Wide Angles and Close-ups

Sidney Mintz, who began fieldwork in Puerto Rico in 1948, describes how, from the air, the southern coastal plains appeared as "an irregular green ribbon" of sugar cane. In the company towns were mills whose "chimneys cast long shadows over the shacks and across the cane." The shacks themselves seemed neat and pretty, in harmony with their surroundings: "the thatched roofs, the waving palms, and the nearness of the sea." This was the view from above. Notice how Mintz conjures strong images through shape, color, and pattern. He then switches to ground level:

> But walking through a village destroys such impressions. The ground is pounded hard and dusty, littered with tin cans, paper, coconut husks and cane trash. The houses are patched with old Coca Cola signs, boards torn from packing cases and cardboard. Only a few are painted. The seeming order dissolves into disorder and crowding. Large families are packed into tight living places. The houses are variously divided into two, three, or more sections by partitions which never reach the ceiling. The cooking is done in ramshackle lean-tos behind the living quarters. And all around the houses grows the cane.

This move from a distanced establishing shot to a close-up echoes the narrative strategy of summary overview and detailed scene. In introducing the sugar cane, the imposing mills, and the shacks crowded around them, Mintz is also preparing readers for the powerful historical and economic forces that shaped the life of his friend Don Taso, the "worker in the cane."

▹ Consider the social practice you are most interested in. Then situate this practice by offering two views: first, a landscape viewed from afar, then a closer view of lived experience.

Mintz goes on to introduce Poblado Jauca, the village in which he conducted his research. He memorably traces how the village changes through the day, from the 5 a.m. stillness and tightly shut windows, through the wakening of the village and the day's busy routines of eating and labor and socializing, to the 9 p.m. quiet on most nights—except for Saturdays after payday. He also describes the rhythms of the week and weekend, of harvest time and the dead time that follows, through to Christmas and the resumption of working in the cane. Beyond these recurring cycles, he points to larger historical shifts. Places, we are reminded, are never still.

▹ Present contrasting images of social life in the same place at different times of day, different times of year, or in different historical eras.

Wide angles and close-ups are also useful in looking around interiors and how they are arranged. Here is Chekhov entering a cell in the Alexandrovsk Hard Labour Prison in Sakhalin. Outside, he noted how neat the prison yard was, and, on first entering the cell, he perceived it as "spacious":

> The windows were open and there was a good deal of light. The walls were unpainted, splintered and dark, with oakum in between the logs; the only things that were white were the tiled dutch stoves. The floor was of wood, unpainted and completely bare. Right the way down the middle of the cell stretched one continuous bed-board, with a slope on both sides, so that the convicts could sleep in two rows, with the heads of one row turned up towards the heads of the other. The convicts' places are not numbered, and are in no way separated from each other, and, owing to this, it's possible to place between seventy and 170 people on the boards.

From this orderly sketch of the general contours of the room and its purpose, and a matter-of-fact enumeration, Chekhov moves without a break to how very uncomfortable, crowded, and chaotic the place is for prisoners:

> There is no bedding whatsoever. Either they sleep on the hard surface, or else underneath themselves they lay torn sacks, their clothing and all sorts of rotting rubbish, extremely off-putting in appearance. On the boards lie caps, boots, bits of bread, empty milk bottles

> stopped up with a bit of paper or old rag, and shoe-trees: under the boards are chests, filthy sacks, bundles, tools and various bits of old clothing. Around the boards is sauntering a well-fed cat. On the walls hang clothes, pots and tools, and on the shelves are teapots, loaves, and boxes of something or other.

Chekhov masterfully undoes the first impression of order with these observations. Describing objects, he also conveys what it would be like to live in the space. The fat, sauntering cat is a classic Chekhovian touch—the detail that seems irrelevant at first, even at odds with the tenor of the rest of the description, and yet, in that very contrast adds to the sense of a living world. For me, the well-fed cat hints at the prisoners' possible generosity even as it suggests rats scurrying through the chaos.

▹ **Describe a room, starting with the layout of space and moving to objects that reveal something about the lives of people who occupy it. Is there a detail that seems out of place, and what might it tell you?**

Chekhov goes on to convey the stench in the Alexandrovsk barracks. As a doctor, he recognizes its similarity to that of hydrogen sulfide and ammoniac. But first, he locates the smells in human practices. The prisoners return from work with wet clothes and dirty boots, hang up some clothes, and bunch up others as makeshift mattresses:

> His sheepskin coat reeks of mutton; his footwear smells of leather and tar. His underwear, permeated with bodily fluids, wet and unwashed, is tossed into a heap along with old sacks and mildewed rags. His footcloths have a suffocating reek of sweat. His body, unwashed, lice-ridden, and flatulent, is addicted to cheap tobacco. Bread, meat, dried fish—which usually he himself salted in prison—crumbs, chunks, bones, and leftover *shchi* all go into his mess tin. He squashes bedbugs with his fingers on the sleeping platform. All this makes for fetid, dank, and sour-smelling prison air.

Notice how Chekhov has expanded on his earlier observations to precisely itemize the sources of bad smell: sheepskin, leather, tar, dirty underwear, old rags, sweaty foot wraps, unwashed flesh, cheap tobacco, farts, bread, meat, salt fish, *shchi* (cabbage soup), bugs. Listing these smells powerfully drives home the conditions under which prisoners were forced to live—laboring, unwashed, wearing rags, and with a poor and unvarying diet.

▹ **Describe the quality of air in a place.**

Painful Places

In a scolding letter to his older, alcoholic brother, written some years before his trip to Sakhalin Island, Chekhov noted that among the traits of decent people is that "they have compassion for other people besides beggars and cats. Their hearts suffer the pain of what is hidden to the naked eye." He seemed to be exhorting his brother to take an imaginative leap into the sources of people's suffering, mentioning among his examples an old couple turning gray and lying awake with worry for an alcoholic son (a perhaps not too oblique reference to their own parents). But this directive to imagine what lies beyond what is immediately visible is also a reminder to describe places that are socially hidden and painful to view—like Sakhalin Island.

Describing the lives of homeless heroin users in San Francisco, Philippe Bourgois and Jeff Schonberg take readers into hidden places in the prosperous city, such as a V-shaped area under a freeway. The book begins with Schonberg's field notes on following two men across an exit ramp to their "shooting gallery" as rush-hour traffic thunders by in both directions:

> A discarded metal generator sits at the far end of the space. Three catty-corner, earthquake reinforced concrete pylons support the double-decker freeways high above us and also shield us from the view of passing cars. My foot sinks into something soft just as Felix warns, "Careful where you step." I move more cautiously now to avoid the other piles of human feces fertilizing the sturdy plants that were selected by freeway planners to withstand a lifetime of car exhaust. The ground is also littered with empty plastic water bottles, candy wrappers, brown paper bags twisted at the stem containing empty bottles of fortified wine, the rusted shards of a metal bed frame and a torn suitcase brimming with discarded clothing. Behind the generator, a sheet of warped plywood rests on a milk crate; on top of the plywood, a Styrofoam cup half full of water and the bottom half of crushed Coke can sit ready for use.
>
> Frank and Felix eagerly hunch over the plywood table and prepare to "fix" a quarter-gram "bag" of Mexican black tar heroin. . . .

The narration then follows every step in the act of shooting up in this largely invisible space. The book combines such descriptions with extensive extracts from interviews and many photographs, unflinchingly documenting the everyday details of subjects' lives while also tracing the violence and inequality embedded in the larger structural forces that have shaped their lives.

▹ Describe some aspect of a place that seems literally or figuratively hidden, and that many people would be likely to ignore or turn away from.

Historically, ethnographers have been drawn to the socially visible, the typical, the routine. Turning to the marginal and the cataclysmic lends a moral force to the enterprise. Though this later gave him nightmares, Chekhov forced himself to bear witness to the brutal flogging of a man known as Vagabond Prokhorov-alias-Mylnikov, who was tied down and lashed ninety times.

Veena Das recalls her visit to a housing block in Delhi in the aftermath of the horrific anti-Sikh riots that occurred after Indira Gandhi was killed by her Sikh bodyguards in 1984. Das shows how grieving women turned the street into "the stage on which a counterstory to the official denial of any wrongdoing could be publicly performed" and describes the "blood spattered on the walls, bullet holes, heaps of ashes in which one could still finds bits of hair or skull and bone." One of these women described her perceptions of the place:

> They have asked us to clean up our houses and go in and settle down. How can we settle down here? Do you see the heaps of ashes? Do you see the blood? Here, put your hand inside this heap and you will see the melted skulls. They would not even let us have the dead bodies. We begged them: you have killed our men. Let us have their bodies at least—let us mourn them properly. The whole night we hear the voices of our dead. I hear my husband asking for water. The killers wouldn't even let us give water to the dying. My son cried, mother, mother—as he used to when he was little, but I could not go to him. This street is now a cremation ground for us. The living have become silent shades, while the cries of the dead float up to the sky and fall on us like weights.

The street, then, had become a memorial to the dead, and the women refused to wash themselves, to clean the place, and to resume routines like cooking.

▹ **Describe a place in the wake of a catastrophic transformation—either natural or political-drawing on direct observation, oral testimony, printed accounts, or photographs.**

The Meeting Place of Texts

Perhaps because I grew up around architects, I think of any piece of writing as a place through which the writer must usher readers. I find myself picturing welcoming doorways, chapter-rooms, window views, closets that suggest hidden secrets. *Sakhalin Island* has a shambling quality, with many mazelike corridors, rooms of different sizes, trapdoors, dank basements, chimneys shooting up—almost as though Chekhov is evading the tsarist censor through the book's complexity.

Chekhov wrote up his Sakhalin materials over the course of several intensely busy years that included travels in Europe, writing short stories and a novella, moving his parents and siblings to the country, organizing famine relief, battling a cholera epidemic, and helping out with the census. Composing within the rigid demands of nonfiction, Chekhov betrayed the impatience of a writer who could usually *invent* the necessary details for short stories and plays. As he complained to his friend Suvorin, he was "forced for the sake of a single mangy line or other to rummage among papers for a full hour."

In a letter written a few years earlier to his brother Alexander, Chekhov had laid out what he considered to be key to a short story:

> 1. absence of lengthy verbiage of political-social-economic nature; 2. total objectivity; 3. truthful descriptions of persons and objects; 4. extreme brevity; 5. audacity and originality: flee the stereotype; 6. compassion.

Keeping *Sakhalin Island* and ethnographic writing more generally in mind, I pondered these points afresh. First, like other ethnographers tracing the larger patterns, structures, processes, and inequalities within which lives are set, in *Sakhalin Island* Chekhov offers extended "political-social-economic" commentaries around specific descriptions—though it's debatable whether these amount to "lengthy verbiage." Second, his call for "total objectivity"—in other letters he expounded further on the writer's need to write as though simply observing lives, without personal judgment—is ironically reversed; if anything, Chekhov can be so frankly judgmental and unflattering in his descriptions of people living in Sakhalin that a contemporary ethnographer squirms. Third, even as he appears to be attempting truthful descriptions, his writing reveals the biases of his particular era, like outdated lens prescriptions. (I'll say more about this in the next chapter.) Fourth, by including so many damning facts, building his case for outrage through the sheer volume of documentation, he is hardly concise—a big contrast to his pared-down stories. Fifth and sixth, here as in his other writings, Chekhov upholds a standard for lasting originality that a writer of any genre might aspire to: writing something different and audacious that cuts through stereotypes and is pervaded by a compassion for people's circumstances.

Nineteen chapters of *Sakhalin Island* were published in serial form in the journal *Russian Thought* in 1893 and 1894. For the complete volume, published in 1895, Chekhov added four more, pointedly critical chapters that hadn't been cleared by the tsarist censors, so running the risk that the book could be withdrawn. Though it's a fiercely critical book, Chekhov managed, by soberly describing what he saw and armoring himself with numbers, to bypass the censors. In its time, *Sakhalin Island* was widely read and resulted in limited reforms. Schools and libraries were built in the settlements, with Chekhov himself leading a drive to send thousands of books. An official commission was sent to Sakhalin to investigate and enact reforms (though in 1905, after the Russo-Japanese war, the southern part of the island was returned to Japan). Chekhov also looked into the possibility of submitting the published book to Moscow University as his dissertation in medicine. Though nothing ever came of his inquiry, after his death a professor at the university wrote that *Sakhalin Island* would become a model "when a department of ethnographical medicine, which we need so much, is opened up."

Chekhov rarely wrote directly of Sakhalin or Siberia in his fiction or plays (the exceptions include powerful stories like "The Murder" and "In Exile"). Yet his encounters with many thousands of people of diverse backgrounds in the course of his Sakhalin census surely crept into the larger canvas of his stories. Reading his harrowing story "Ward No. 6," set in a hospital ward for mental patients, after the description of smells in the Sakhalin Island prison barracks, it's hard not to notice similarities: in an outer area, "mattresses, old torn dressing gowns, trousers, blue-striped shirts, worn-out shoes—all these rags are piled in heaps, crumpled, tangled, rotting, and giving out a suffocating smell"—while inside, "there is a stench of pickled cabbage, charred wicks, bedbugs and ammonia . . ." It's no surprise to learn that Chekhov wrote this story in 1892, when he was also working on *Sakhalin Island*.

A few years later, when a politically active student in Saint Petersburg was sentenced to ten years on Sakhalin, his older brother wrote asking Chekhov for help. Chekhov wrote back to this older brother, David Manucharov, saying that though he no longer knew people in Sakhalin he would try to intervene through connections in Petersburg. Chekhov explained that he hadn't been allowed to meet alone with political prisoners but shared what little he knew about their condition. Since Manucharov was considering whether he should find work in Sakhalin to be near his brother, Chekhov also offered advice on how he might apply for a job as a senior supervisor at a workshop. Chekhov ends his first letter to the distraught Manucharov with the observation that a place need not entirely dictate the sort of person living there:

> Reassure your brother; tell him even on Sakhalin there are good people who will not turn away from giving him help and advice.
>
> I send you my best wishes, and am at your service,
>
> Your
> A. Chekhov

* · * · * · * · * · * · * · * · * · * · * · * · * · * · * · * · * · * · * · *

PLACE

Set the stage for an event you want to describe. Include, in any order, at least passing mentions of the season, place-names, the landscape, the built environment, and (if applicable) an interior. Work with all of your senses. 2 pages.

THREE Person

In *Reading Chekhov: A Critical Journey*, Janet Malcolm observes, "In Russia, no less than in our country, possibly even more than in our country, Chekhov attracts a kind of sickening piety. You utter the name Chekhov and people arrange their features as if a baby deer had come into the room."

The first time I read Malcolm's wonderful book I was amused by this passage; the second time, having fallen under Chekhov's spell, I marked those lines. I paused, sorting out for myself the forces that swirl together in the powerful aura around his name—if not outright piety, at least a compelling connection. I remembered how I'd encountered Chekhov's name some years earlier in Kangra, Northwest India. A bright, animated village girl a few years younger than me yet already far beyond the usual marriageable age for the region, had mentioned Chekhov as we sat talking in her family's courtyard.

She had found discarded copies of a Soviet publication in Hindi amid stacks of old newspapers and magazines that a tailor used to wrap up clothes. Reading Chekhov's stories in translation, she said, had so moved her that she had begun teaching herself Russian from this magazine, *Soviat Nari* (Soviet Woman). My friend's hushed invocation of Chekhov's name had seemed to me a coded way to hint at a forceful imaginative pull toward wider horizons and greater possibilities than her life then allowed. For as Malcolm points out, while Chekhov seems to write reassuring realism, he is often showing up life's surreal and ecstatic moments.

Is it partly Chekhov's sympathy for his characters' longings that draws readers across time and space to perceive him as speaking very directly, personally, to them? Perhaps. Yet as Malcolm so masterfully shows as she weaves together biography, literary criticism, and travelogue, people respond to Chekhov not just because of his imaginative creations, but also because of their perceptions of the kind of person he was.

We glimpse Chekhov in his writings and in the ever-widening river of writings about him. Dipping into this literature, I found myself fixated by the observations of Chekhov's consociates: the people who chatted with him, watched him waste away with illness, laughed with him as he threw his head back and flung off his pince-nez. In the years following his death and especially after the enormous upheavals of the Russian Revolution of 1917, reminiscences of Chekhov were written by his relatives, his friends, and his fellow writers—some of them now in exile. Despite the elegiac, nostalgic tone that pervades many of the reminiscences, in reading them I discovered details that pulled Chekhov into vivid presence. In this chapter, as I offer strategies for describing people, I draw on descriptions of Chekhov and also a few other unforgettable people I have encountered in memoirs and ethnographies.

Describing other people is a big challenge, whatever the form you choose. If you're frank, you risk offending another person by drawing attention to something that he or she might prefer not be mentioned at all, and especially not in print: for example, a less than perfect aspect of their physical appearance, comportment, way of relating to others, or background. They may be offended; worse, they could be harmed. Photographs can be superbly evocative, filling in details without your having to resort to words, but less than flattering photographs can also cause tensions; then too, photographs can reveal identities, even when captions are couched in the most general possible terms. If institutional guidelines for research involving human subjects have committed you to using pseudonyms, mentioning what seems most characteristic about a person could knock aside your most dutiful efforts to mask identity. You may try to protect people by creating composite characters, but such rearranging must be done carefully so that these composites remain socially grounded even as they become fictional inventions. None of these problems can be settled in the abstract: you have to rethink them afresh for every project, every person, and through sequences of written drafts.

Your project probably involves many people—some presented as complex and surprisingly "round" characters, in E. M. Forster's terms, with other, comparatively flat supporting characters in the background. I'll focus here on "round" representation while urging you to consider how using unexpected words or details might also bring memorable color to background characters. Drawing up a list of people you hope to include can help you sort through whom you'll foreground (and help keep straight any pseudonyms you might use).

▹ Make a list of people you hope to write about, with a line or two of description after each name.

This list might shrink or expand as the project unfolds. Some ethnographies that involve lots of characters include a list of characters with brief summaries of their roles and relationships, like the dramatis personae at the start of theatrical scripts. Even if you don't include such a section in your published work, notice for yourself as you look over the list what aspects of these people's lives you found most immediately worth mentioning.

Types and Individuals

Much social scientific writing contains people within social categories or types, while fiction and creative nonfiction more commonly follow very particular individuals and their concerns. Ethnographic writing blends these perspectives in different measures, depending on the form. Even the most general of ethnographies about a group of people, whether the Trobrianders, the Tikopia, or the Azande, calls attention to some individuals in anecdotes. At the other end of the spectrum, even life histories—an ethnographic blend of autobiography and biography, most often focusing on a single person—usually situate the person's story by alluding to shared patterns of experience. Through ethnography, I've come to better appreciate how people, myself included, live within the shaping constraints of larger shared structures even as we maneuver within or around these constraints and at times actively transform the structures. I also continue looking for ways to evoke the distinctive quirkiness of individuals.

Writing about Sakhalin, Chekhov worked partly within his era's ethnographic conventions, where individuals were largely subsumed by typification. Particularly in sections describing the plight of the indigenous Gilyak and Ainu under colonization, he follows the shorthand of prior authors in listing "typical" distinguishing bodily features, outfits, character traits, and forms of social organization. When he moves to individuals—recounting, for example, a conversation with two Gilyak men who were curious about him—the element of caricature starts to fall away. But as is the case with most fleeting encounters, he still doesn't convey a sense of them on their *own* terms. Writing about more ethnically familiar convict and settler men and women from mainland Russia, he can also generalize in unflattering ways, but he seems better able to make sense of their specificity. Yet when he talks at length with someone, his empathy and eye for detail bring the person to life on the page. For example, here is the convict "Krasivy Family-forgotten" steering the square box that served as a ferry across the river:

> He was already seventy-one years old. Hunchbacked, shoulder blades protruding, one rib broken, a thumb missing, his whole body was covered with scars and lashings suffered a long time ago. He had almost no gray hair; his hair seemed faded, his eyes were blue, sparkling and he wore a happy, good-natured expression. He was dressed in rags and was barefoot.

Krasivy tells Chekhov how he had landed in this situation: for deserting the tsarist army, then running away when he was sentenced to Siberia. He had been in Sakhalin for twenty-two years and had mostly managed to live peacefully by always following orders and holding to his philosophy: "To tell the truth and not anger God, life is good! Glory to Thee, O Lord!"

The finer grain of such descriptions reminds us why ethnographic methods emphasize living with people over time and conversing with them in their own languages. But what sort of insights about other people emerge from coexistence that extends far beyond any demarcated project? Memoirs, for example, often draw on years—even an entire lifetime—of informal participant observation.

I reflected on what ethnography might gain from memoir when I read Paul Auster's account of his father, "Portrait of an Invisible Man." Auster began recording these memories in the weeks after his father's sudden death. Sorting through his father's possessions, he also sorted through memories. Auster evokes his father through many disparate images, "each one, in itself, a fleeting resurrection, a moment otherwise lost." He recalls how his father walked and ate, the smells of his father's car, and particular moments together. Then he moves on to a list with the powerful cadences of a poem:

> The size of his hands. Their calluses.
>
> Eating the skin off the top of hot chocolate.
>
> Tea with lemon.
>
> The pairs of black, horn-rimmed glasses scattered through the house: on kitchen counters, on table tops, at the edge of the bathroom sink—always open, lying there like some strange unclassified form of animal.
>
> Watching him play tennis.
>
> The way his knees sometimes buckled when he walked.
>
> His face.
>
> His resemblance to Abraham Lincoln, and how people always remarked on it.
>
> His fearlessness with dogs.
>
> His face. And again, his face.
>
> Tropical fish.

Auster's list suggested a writing prompt that I've since used in both ethnographic writing classes and memoir workshops.

▹ Choose a person you consider central to your work and take Auster's swift sketch as a model to start describing her or him. You could follow Auster's structure—which I've generalized here to a list of categories—or improvise on whatever sequence helps you start writing:

an arresting physical detail

a quirky habit

signature food or drink

object(s) associated with the person

an activity you observed

the person in motion

a feature that holds presence

a resemblance, if any

a trait evoked in interaction

a hobby or delight.

Students and workshop participants have written about just about anyone they've had a chance to observe closely—family members, best friends, roommates, romantic partners, and even someone they know from prior fieldwork. This exercise, I've found, churns up feelings about the person described, and sometimes, reading the list aloud, the writer's voice catches. As participants share their pieces, the number of people present in the room begins to double. We sense not just the quirky individuality of the people described, but also the idiosyncratic sensibilities of their observers.

Here is what I came up with for Chekhov, based on the recollections of his friends, relatives, and fellow writers:

> The iris of his right eye brighter than his left.
>
> Intently listening, fingers picking at his beard.
>
> Medicines prescribed, medicines consumed, medicines commemorated by the family dogs Quinine and Bromide.
>
> In later life, a wire-rimmed pince-nez that he raised his chin to look through.
>
> Watching him racked by coughing.
>
> The way he smiled in a sudden flash.
>
> Chestnut-dark hair combed back from his forehead.
>
> His resemblance to black-and-white photographs of his own dashing, then dwindling, selves.
>
> His elusiveness with female admirers.
>
> Funny stories.

Next, to illustrate the mutually illuminating relation between individuals and groups, switch from details to generalizations.

▹ **Make the widest general statement of the person as a "type," putting an emphasis on the category of most interest to your project, showing simultaneously how the person fits and diverges from this category.**

My own freewritten paragraph, written alongside students in a workshop, began: "Anton Pavlovitch Chekhov stands among the great nineteenth-century Russian writers. He only inhabited the first few years of the twentieth century, as he died in 1904. Unlike most of those other Great Russian Writers who wrote thick books, when writing fiction, Chekhov mostly stayed within the short story form that could be stretched toward a novella . . ." And so on.

The Embodied Person

We usually perceive others first through their bodily presence. Here is how K. Korovin, an artist who was studying with Chekhov's friend Levitan, described meeting Chekhov in Moscow in 1883. They were all students at the time, and Chekhov was twenty-three years old:

> Anton Pavlovich's room was full of tobacco smoke, and a samovar was standing on the table. There were also small loaves of bread, sausage and beer. The divan was covered with sheets of paper and college notebooks—Anton was preparing for his medical finals at the university.
>
> He was sitting on the edge of the divan and wearing a grey jacket of the kind many students wore in those days. There were some other young people in the room, students.
>
> The students were talking and arguing heatedly, drinking tea and beer and eating sausage. Anton Pavlovich sat in silence, only occasionally replying to questions addressed to him.
>
> He was handsome with a large open face and kindly, laughing eyes. When conversing with someone, he would sometimes gaze into his face, but then immediately drop his head and give a curious, gentle smile.

Chekhov had already been writing as "Antosha Chekhonte" for a few years, supplementing his university stipend with short and funny pieces for newspapers and magazines. Notice how he is set in a room, identified as part of a group of students through his papers, notebooks, gray jacket, comrades, and eating habits.

▹ Describe a first impression, physically locating someone in reference to a social group, whether through objects, appearance, dress, habits, or interactions.

Of course, the categories you draw on to situate a person might change with perspective and unfolding life trajectories: Chekhov could variously be described not just amid students, but also doctors, writers, playwrights. He might be placed in terms of his ancestry and class background. Or he might be located in terms of places he lived for long stretches—his hometown of Taganrog, Moscow, Melikhovo (in the countryside outside Moscow), or Yalta, the southern holiday town by the Black Sea, where he built a house when his tuberculosis made living in Moscow a challenge. He might also be linked to places he wrote about, which would include Sakhalin.

Olga Knipper, the vibrant leading actress in the Moscow Art Theater, registered a different first impression of Chekhov. Knipper knew Chekhov only in the last six years of his life, when he was already a celebrated literary figure and, as she later remembered, "growing weaker in health and stronger in spirit." They first met in 1898, when he visited the theater group for a rehearsal of his controversial play *The Seagull* (which I will return to later in this chapter). Knipper recalled that the actors were in a flurry of excitement to meet him. When Chekhov appeared—the open face Korovin had described fifteen years earlier now transformed by a beard and glasses—they did not know what to say:

> And he looked at us, now smiling, now grave, with something like shyness, plucking at his little beard and toying with his pince-nez, and turning suddenly to examine some antique vases that were being made for the production of Antigone.
>
> When asked a question, he would give an unexpected reply that seemed somehow beside the point, so that at first one did not quite know whether he was speaking seriously or in jest. But the next moment the seemingly casual remark would penetrate one's mind and heart and a mere hint would be enough to throw light on the essence of a character.

Knipper made a strong impression on Chekhov when he saw her onstage in a different play just before his return to Yalta; he confessed in a letter to Suvorin that the performance had brought a lump to his throat, and had he remained in Moscow, he'd have fallen in love with the character she played. Knipper and Chekhov's connection would blossom with subsequent meetings and through a flirtatious correspondence.

Despite the gap in years between these two descriptions, notice how Knipper's account of Chekhov's apparent bashfulness and mobile features echoes Korovin's description of him as a student.

▹ If you've known someone through time, focus for a moment on traits that have endured and describe the person's habitual gestures.

Knipper also noted Chekhov's fidgeting and that he seemed a little out of kilter in conversation. Others too remarked on his apparent absentmindedness, almost as though he was simultaneously interacting with people and turning inward, toward the making of stories.

Chekhov's mother Yevgenia recalled him as a student: "Antosha would sit at the table in the morning, having his tea and suddenly fall to thinking; he would sometimes look straight into one's eyes, but I knew that he saw nothing. Then he would get his note-book out of his pocket and write quickly, quickly. And again he would fall to thinking." His younger sister Masha, who devoted much of her life to supporting his work and later his memory, also described how he could be physically transformed when possessed by a story that had yet to be written:

> His way of walking and his voice changed, a sort of absent-mindedness appeared, and he often answered questions at random. He usually looked a bit odd at these times. This continued until the moment he began writing, when he became his old self again: obviously the theme and images had now fully matured, and his creative tension was ending.

Writers aren't just momentarily transformed by creative trances; some also carry lasting physical effects from their work, whether aching wrists, sore shoulders, or strained vision.

Consider, with respect to your own project, how bodies might be marked by the work they perform, whether activities like Chekhov's or heavier physical labor. Here is how Sidney Mintz first introduces Don Taso, the subject of the life history *Worker in the Cane*:

> I recall how Taso looked that first afternoon. He was slight of build but his arms were heavily muscled and very tanned; his hands seemed almost grotesque, for he is a small-boned delicate man, and his hands would have looked fitting on a person twice his weight and size. His face was very wrinkled; when I found out later how young he really was I was shocked by the disparity I thought I saw between his age and his appearance. He had no teeth, and used a pair of badly fitting dentures with a lot of gold in them. He wore a white shirt—the badge of dignity of the Puerto Rican worker at rest—a rather natty but worn cream-colored fedora, shoes but no socks.

Notice Mintz's use of telling physical details as he concisely establishes how a body carries signs of physical labor and how clothes establish class.

▹ Describe a person's body as marked by her or his occupation and activities.

Bodies change. Those who knew Chekhov well were alarmed as he became frail, his sturdy good looks diminished by the advancing tuberculosis. His famous story "The Lady with the Little Dog" carries a scene that poignantly acknowledges the marks of age. Written in 1899, at a time when Chekhov and Knipper were romantically involved, this story includes a moment in winter, in a Moscow hotel room, where the married but womanizing Dmitri Gurov stands before a mirror with his hands on the warm shoulders of his younger, married lover Anna Sergeyevna, whom he is consoling. He had begun the affair to pass the time when they met at a resort in Yalta. Months later, as he observes his reflection, "it seemed strange to him that he had aged so much in those last years, had lost so much of his good looks," and that "only now, when his head was gray, had he really fallen in love as one ought to—for the first time in his life." It's hard not to read these lines and wonder if they might echo a moment when the thirty-nine-year-old Chekhov had glimpsed his own reflection over his own younger lover's shoulders. But also, the passage is a reminder of how, set within a skillfully told story, even a spare description can conjure a powerful image.

In her ethnography of a Jewish senior citizen center in Venice Beach, California, Barbara Myerhoff writes with memorable and compassionate detail about the effects of aging on bodies. Among the elderly people she came to know during her research in the late

1960s and early 1970s was Shmuel Goldman, a retired tailor, who often didn't get along with others at the center. Here is how Myerhoff describes Shmuel, when he was eighty and his wife Rebekah, was seventy-four:

> Time had sharpened his facial planes, paring off all nonessential flesh. The lips were a thin neutral line, the eyes deep and close together, unclouded by cataracts or glaucoma. His smile was restrained and rare. Only his hair and ears and cheekbones were exuberant. His teeth were jagged and stained but they were his own. I liked them and realized how depressing I found the false white sameness of the others' dentures. The cables of his neck wired his great, gaunt head onto a springy, tidy frame.
>
> Rebekah came to the couch and sat down next to Shmuel. She too had her own teeth and, like him, lacked the equipment that makes so many among the elderly look alike at first glance—the heavy glasses, hearing aids, dentures. Rebekah was also small, energetic, and erect. Even their hands were the same size, the backs blotched with brown spots; but the fingers were uncrimped by arthritis.

Notice how these descriptions establish what you might expect someone of a certain age to look like within a particular cultural setting, and also celebrate the distinctiveness of Shmuel and Rebekah's appearance.

▹ Describe someone with reference to their gender- and age-mates in a particular setting.

People don't always care to reveal their exact age. You might experiment with obliquely establishing approximate age not by citing years but through passing details slipped into description—gray streaks at the temples, the unfolding of reading glasses, the startled gaze that can follow plastic surgery, the presence of grown children and grandchildren or recollections of dated events.

Lives Told by Things

A person's cherished objects can reveal aspects of her or his biography and values. Myerhoff describes how Shmuel showed her a poem he had written in Yiddish that began, "God's greatest invention, / A little needle, / Humble, bright and quick." He regarded his work as a tailor as both a service that connected him to others and an expression of his own creativity. Because of Jewish tailors like himself, he said, people in America who weren't particularly wealthy had been able to afford coats. He shared his philosophy of work: "The mind must be alive when you sew, if you are in a good shop or a bad. . . . The outside conditions do not apply. You must bring it up from the inside, looking always for a way to express yourself." On another occasion he said:

> The work has no beginning and no end, but a story is told, it grows on in the head. A needle goes in and out. You hold a thread in your fingers. It goes to the garment, to the fingers, to the one who wears the garment, all connected. This is what matters, not whether you are paid for what you do.

▹ **How does the person you're writing about describe the meaning of material objects central to a sense of self? How might these objects connect this person to others?**

The association between Shmuel and tailoring was so strong that after he died, his friend Abe Beidleman compared Shmuel himself to a well-made garment, and a needle too. Shmuel, he said, was

> like a fine cloak, everything well-stitched together, good strong seams, cloth not fine but not cheap, long-lasting. Himself, he was also like a needle—sharp, practical, quick, jabbing people sometimes because that was necessary.

What a gift to an ethnographer when another person can supply a description this eloquent! It's a strong reminder, too, to listen attentively to how people describe each other and to include their words in your own attempts at description. Beidleman's drawing on Shmuel Goldman's profession suggests a prompt:

▹ **Compare a person to an object with which their life's work is closely connected: "______ is like [or not like] a ______."**

Simply listing a person's things can create a powerful cumulative impression. I think for example, of James Agee's lists in *Let Us Now Praise Famous Men*, as he documents the lives of three families of poor tenant farmers in Alabama during the Depression. Room by spare room, he lists and describes objects; item by worn item, he describes family members' clothing. But lists, I think, are most effective in small doses: it takes a truly brilliant writer to sustain a readers' interest across many lists. In most cases, slipping in details as parts of an unfolding narrative may work better.

As I looked around for an example for a prompt in which clothing or décor appears in the background, I remembered a scene written by my younger self in which Swamiji, an old holy man in Western India, was recounting his life story. Swamiji's chosen deity was the mother goddess in the form of Saptashring Nivasini Devi—a large-eyed, coral-complexioned, eighteen-armed goddess—whose mountaintop temple he had lived near for some years:

> "From childhood, were you a devotee of the Goddess?" was my opening question. Swamiji was leaning against the wall on his bed, legs resting on a stool before him. A pink mosquito net was hooped over his head. I sat on the floor at his feet. He looked past me to the altar on the opposite wall where there was a color picture of Saptashring Nivasini Devi, silver sandals belonging to his Guru, a picture of his Guru, a silver square inscribed with a geometrical *shree yantrā* (representing the Goddess)—and with Swamiji's flair for improvisation, a globe and clouded mirror. Bowing to the altar, my head had grazed Africa and then I had confronted myself through a pearly haze.
>
> "*Hān*? What?" My question took a moment to sink in.

I remember writing this scene as a graduate student, trying to convey Swamiji's zany informality through the surprising setting: the footstool in front of the bed, the gauzy pink canopy of mosquito net. Since the life story he had gone on to tell was mostly of his quest for spiritual meaning, it made sense to describe the objects, sacred to him, that were placed idiosyncratically on his altar.

▹ List a person's objects that are relevant to the themes you're trying to express. Then write a few sentences situating the person in relation to them.

Inner Biography

What's the central imaginative project in another person's life? This could be the same as a person's livelihood, or it might be very different. In an early collection of portraits of anthropologists' "key informants," Victor Turner recalls his friend Muchona in what was then Rhodesia and is now Zimbabwe. Turner introduces Muchona, whom he has met walking along a dusty road, as a "swart elderly gnome who was padding perkily beside us." When Turner asked him about medicines, Muchona replied "readily and at length, with the bright glance of the true enthusiast. He had a high-pitched voice, authoritative as a school-teacher's when conveying information, expressive as a comedian's when telling a tale." Though Muchona was the son of a slave from another tribe, had a tendency to drink too much, and was at the margins of Ndembu society, he was enormously knowledgeable about Ndembu ritual healing. (This portrait reveals Turner's marvelous essays on Ndembu ritual symbolism to be partly Muchona's exegetical creations.) As Turner writes:

> In the main, the pattern of his personality, like that of a poet in his poem, expressed itself in his accounts and interpretations of ritual, and in the nuances of gesture, expression and phrase with which he embellished them. In a sense therefore, Muchona's ritual history is his inner biography, for in ritual he found his deepest satisfactions.

▹ Using the concept of "inner biography," can you point to a significant theme of creative engagement in a person's life?

Chekhov seems to hint at a similar disjuncture in "The Lady with the Little Dog": as Gurov is taking his daughter to school on his way to the tryst with Anna Sergeevna, he reflects that what the people around him know about his respectable married and professional life is just a shell, concealing what most matters. The critic James Wood expresses this beautifully: "In Chekhov's world, our inner lives run at their own speed. . . . In his stories the free inner life bumps against the outer life like two different time-systems, like the Julian calendar against the Gregorian." While a fiction writer can freely imagine and describe this inner life, an ethnographer is constrained, in Gurov's terms, to staying at the level of what people choose to reveal.

Chekhov's own "inner biography" would seem partly revealed in the compassionate sweep of his writings—the exact conjunctions can't fully be known. But those who remembered him did describe his writing as an activity that shaped his outward life: how he could, even when he was in company, seem to withdraw inward or muse alone; how he could take shelter in the next room when too many visitors showed up with their demands; how he distanced himself from most women who were becoming too close. At the same time, sociable connection shaped his life as a writer. He could be gregarious, charming, and funny, a prankster, a flirt, a connoisseur of absurd stories, and a host to many diverse guests.

The writer Alexander Kuprin describes this tension in Chekhov's daily routine during the period when declining health had forced him away from the Moscow cold to the balmy climate of Yalta. In the summer, Kuprin recalled, Chekhov would rise very early, dress immaculately, and get to work in his study. But his solitary creativity was disrupted later in the day by swarms of visitors, including female admirers (who in a play on a variety of winter apple called *antonovska*, became known as the *antonovski*):

> Evidently, his best time for work was in the morning before lunch, although nobody ever managed to find him writing: in this respect he was extraordinarily reserved and shy. All the same, on nice warm mornings he could be seen sitting on a slope behind the house, in the cosiest part of the place, where oleanders stood in tubs along the walls, and where he had planted a cypress. There he sat sometimes for an hour or longer, alone, without stirring, with his hands on his knees, looking in front of him at the sea.
>
> At midday and later visitors began to fill the house. Girls stood for hours at the iron railings, separating the bungalow from the road, with open mouths, in white felt hats. The most diverse people came to Chekhov: scholars, authors, Zemstvo [rural administrative] workers, doctors, military, painters, admirers of both sexes, professors, society men and women, senators, priests, actors—and God knows who else. Often he was asked to give advice or help and still more often to give his opinion upon manuscripts. Casual newspaper reporters and people who were merely inquisitive would appear; also people who came to him with the sole purpose of "directing the big, but erring talent to the proper, ideal side." Beggars came—genuine and sham. These never met with a refusal. . . . I know for certain that Chekhov's generosity towards students of both sexes was immeasurably beyond what his modest means would allow.

These passages moved me, I think, partly because of the extreme contrasts: the self-contained quiet of Chekhov emerging from his study to muse at the sea, hands on his knees, and the great diverse hubbub of visitors with their demands. I was reminded again of how contrast enlivens description.

▹ Following the theme of creative engagement, juxtapose two moments of solitary absorption and social interaction.

When his friend Suvorin urged him to marry in 1895, Chekhov responded by letter that he couldn't bear the thought of a wife who would be around all the time; he would prefer to live in the country while she lived in Moscow. "I promise to be a splendid husband," he wrote, "but let me have a wife who, like the moon, will not appear in my sky everyday." In an aside, he added, "Having a wife won't make me write any better." He found waxing and waning companionability in Olga Knipper. After they married in the summer of 1901, she continued acting in Moscow and he remained mostly in Yalta, some eight hundred miles away. Through their long separations, they wrote long letters. They both hoped to have a child, but this did not happen.

Knipper was vacationing with Chekhov in a German resort when his body gave way to complications from tuberculosis. Her memories of their last day together include Chekhov's famous final words: "It's a long time since I drank champagne." A doctor summoned at night had ordered this champagne as a professional courtesy on recognizing another doctor who was dying; in Knipper's account, Chekhov smiled at her, said those words, drained the glass of cold champagne, lay back on his left side, and died.

Nonhuman Persons

Knipper's account also mentions how, in the quiet after Chekhov's last breath, a big black moth burst into the room, banging about against the lamps. She describes this without interpretation, but as an anthropologist I couldn't help thinking of other cultures in which such a moth might be seen as a counterpart to Chekhov's spirit. Many cultures attribute qualities of personhood to nonhuman categories of being: deities, spirits, animals, plants, objects, natural formations, institutions, even diseases. Ethnography can convey such nonhuman persons from the perspectives of those who are interacting with them.

Here is a selection from Karen McCarthy Brown's *Mama Lola*, about a Vodou priestess in Brooklyn. At a birthday party of the Azaka—a *lwa*, or Vodou spirit—on Memorial Day weekend, Mama Lola, also known as Alourdes, led a group of worshippers that included her daughter Maggie in summoning Azaka. The center of high energy,

Aloudes sang, danced, and saluted the altar. Eventually, Azaka arrived:

> Her body shuddered and jerked, went lax for a moment, and then jerked again rapidly. These movements mark the struggles between the *lwa* and Alourdes's *gwo bònanj* (big guardian angel) who ordinarily presides, "in her head." When the spirit wins the contest (it almost always does), the *gwo bònanj* is sent from the body to wander, as it does routinely during sleep, and Alourdes becomes the *chwal* (horse) of the spirit. Several people moved around Alourdes to help her, but there was no urgency in their movement; no one thought she was in danger. Indeed, many people in the room seemed to take no special note of her, as if the events were in no way unusual or remarkable.
>
> Her shoes were removed and with one person supporting her under each arm, Azaka's blue scarf was tied around her neck The first sign that Azaka was seated firmly on his horse was his high-pitched nasal chirp: "whooooo, whooooo . . . whooooo . . . whoooop!" Maggie reached for the voluminous blue denim shirt made especially for Azaka and struggled to put it on him. Then she put his straw hat on his head and hung his *makout* (straw satchel) over one shoulder. . . .
>
> "*Bonswa, Kompè. Bonswa, ti Kouzinn* [Good evening, Brother. Good evening, little Cousin]," Azaka said, speaking in the highly nasal voice characteristic of peasant speech. Then he looked timidly around the room from beneath the brim of his straw hat.

Notice how Brown shifts pronouns as the body of Mama Lola becomes the "horse" for Azaka to ride into presence. A change in costume enhances the transformation, and Brown shows also how Mama Lola's forceful personality and usual speaking style is replaced by the presence of a timid male peasant.

▹ Describe a moment of doubling, where someone is both the person you know and someone else, for example, a character in a performance, a deity, a spirit, a virtual "avatar." Note the gestures, props, and voice shifts.

Similarly, Rane Willerslev's *Soul Hunters* opens out the boundaries of personhood by describing how the Yukaghir of Siberia perceive mimetic doublings among humans, animals, and spirits. The book opens with a Yukaghir man dressed up as an elk on skis, yet carrying a gun as he approaches a female elk:

> Watching old Spiridon rocking his body back and forth, I was puzzled whether the figure I saw before me was a man or elk. The elk-hide coat worn with its hair outward, the headgear with its characteristic protruding ears, and the skis covered with an elk's smooth leg skins, so as to sound like the animal when moving in snow, made him an elk; yet the lower part of his face below the hat, with its human eyes, nose, and mouth, along with the loaded rifle in his hands, made him a man. Thus, it was not that Spiridon had stopped being human. Rather, he had a liminal quality: he was not an elk, and yet he was also not *not* an elk. He was occupying a strange place in between human and nonhuman identities.
>
> A female elk appeared from among the willow bushes with her offspring. At first the animals stood still, the mother lifting and lowering her huge head in bewilderment, unable to solve the puzzle in front of her. But as Spiridon moved closer, she was captured by his mimetic performance, suspended her disbelief, and started walking straight toward him with the calf trotting behind her. At that point he lifted his gun and shot them both dead. Later he explained the incident: "I saw two persons dancing toward me. The mother was a beautiful young woman and while singing, she said: 'Honored friend. Come and I'll take you by the arm and lead you to our home.' At that point I killed them both. Had I gone with her, I myself would have died. She would have killed me."

This passage gains dramatic force partly through the shifts in perspective: how Spiridon appeared to the ethnographer; how Spiridon seemed to appear to the female elk; and what Spiridon reported seeing, which was not visible to the ethnographer.

▹ Draw on a perspective other than your own to describe a moment that a person appeared as both human and nonhuman.

Imagining across Time

Much ethnography draws on fieldnotes. How does a writer include moments that may never have found their way into notes or photographs, that might rely on secondhand accounts, and yet have left a lingering image in memory or imagination? In *The High Valley*, a popular narrative ethnography of his research in New Guinea in the early 1950s, Kenneth Read took a daring leap toward describing a moment at which he was not present, but which proved key to his association with the Gahuku highland tribes. His future friend, the charismatic headman Makis, had walked into a colonial district office to request a white man for the tribe. By chance, on the assistant district officer's desk was a letter from Read asking help in finding a place for research. Read later recreated this pivotal moment for his research:

> I can imagine Makis entering the office with his flair for coloring everything he did with drama, appearing first of all in the rectangle of sunlight beyond the doorway, a dark silhouette set within a nimbus of brightness that momentarily extinguished the shadows as he stepped across the threshold and came to attention in the approved manner, the movement of his arm, lifted in a smart salute, causing his ornaments of shell to clash and jingle bravely. In later months he often appeared before me in this manner when I was working alone at night, materializing suddenly in the hissing glare of my kerosene, or tilley, lamp and filling the whole room with his presence.

This passage forcefully ricochets between the imagined moment and the grounded memories, each reinforcing the other.

▹ Describe a person at a moment that you did not witness but were told about later, starting with "I can imagine . . ." (You might also point to the source of the image.)

Moments when we actually were present can also be emblazoned in memory, forming images that we return to again without quite knowing why. Here is a scene from V. I. Nemirovich-Danchenko's account of Chekhov. Nemirovich-Danchenko was a writer who founded the Moscow Art Theater with Constantin Stanislavski (he is also thought to have been involved with Olga Knipper). He takes credit for having first suggested a piece of advice about following through on details that is often attributed to Chekhov: that a loaded gun introduced by the end of a play's first act must be eventually fired. Chekhov had sought out Nemirovich-Danchenko's advice on his manuscript for *The Seagull*—a play that even in manuscript was being severely critiqued for its departure from conventional form. As Nemirovich-Danchenko offered suggestions, Chekhov listened:

> I cannot explain why his image, as I analyzed his play in detail and at length, so imprinted itself on my memory. I was sitting at my desk, the manuscript in front of me, and he was standing by the window, his back to me, his hands, as always, in his pockets. He did not turn

> round once, at least for a whole half hour, and did not say a single word. There was not the slightest doubt that he was listening to me with particular attention, yet at the same time it was as if he was carefully following something happening in the little garden in front of the windows of my apartment; sometimes he even moved closer to the glass to look through, and turned his head slightly. Was this a desire to make it easier for me to speak freely, not embarrass me by catching my eye, or, on the contrary, was it to preserve his own dignity?

For me, the haunting power of this description lies partly in its open-endedness. Nemirovich-Danchenko doesn't pretend to know what was going on inside Chekhov's head and doesn't attempt to explain what made this moment so indelible. Instead of containing Chekhov, and his memory, with a single interpretation, Nemirovich-Danchenko allows for a range of complex reasons opened up through questions.

▹ **Describe a person in a scene fixed in your memory. Allow your understanding of that moment to remain a set of unresolved questions.**

The Seagull opened in Saint Petersburg in October 1896. A well-known comic actress, Elizaveta Levkeyeva, had chosen the play as the first performance of an evening to celebrate the twenty-fifth anniversary of her career. The audience had expected a comedy and began loudly talking, laughing, coughing, heckling, as the acts moved forward. Another actress later recalled glimpsing Levkeyeva and Chekhov backstage between acts. Levkeyeva was "looking at him with an expression either of guilt or of sympathy in her prominent eyes," while Chekhov was "sitting with his head slightly bowed, a lock of hair had fallen down over his forehead, and his pince-nez was resting lopsidedly on the bridge of his nose. . . . Neither of them said a word."

Chekhov's disheartened posture sums up why he walked out of the theater to wander the city. He left Saint Petersburg the next day, resolving never again to write plays. It wasn't until a full two years later that his friend Nemirovitch-Danchenko insisted on putting *The Seagull* on at the Moscow Art Theater. This time the play was a resounding success, though Chekhov, who was by then in Yalta, did not attend the opening night. His reputation as a playwright was retrieved. The Moscow Art Theater went on to stage *Uncle Vanya* (a substantially transformed version of his earlier play *The Wood Demon*), and Chekhov also wrote two new plays for the group: *The Three Sisters* and *The Cherry Orchard*.

Writing over a century later, I have the advantage of knowing that these plays by Chekhov are read, performed, and adapted to this day. Chekhov's contemporaries' accounts of his silences—standing by the window as *The Seagull* was critiqued, sitting backstage as it opened—remind me again of the power of scenes. A scene depicting a person's vulnerability when stranded within a messily unfurling story can communicate more about that person than a summary that tidily wraps up how things turned out.

* · *

PERSON

Introduce a person—in a scene or through a portrait. Observe his or her appearance, mannerisms, social location. Try to indicate—through implicit showing or explicit telling—how his or her life was affected by the central theme in which you are interested. 2 pages.

FOUR Voice

Assembling different accounts of Anton Chekhov from his contemporaries, I was especially struck by Maxim Gorky's memories. Why? I reread, trying to understand. From the very first paragraphs, Chekhov speaks. Gorky begins by recalling his visit to Chekhov when he was living in a Tatar village near the resort of Yalta, on the Black Sea:

> He once invited me to visit him in the village of Kuchuk-Koi, where he had a tiny plot of land and a white, two-storey house. He showed me over his "estate," talking animatedly all the time.
>
> "If I had lots of money I would build a sanatorium here for sick village teachers. A building full of light, you know, very light, with big windows and high ceilings. I'd have a splendid library, all sorts of musical instruments, an apiary, a vegetable garden, an orchard. I'd have lectures on agronomy, meteorology, and so on—teachers ought to know everything, old man, everything!"

> He broke off suddenly, coughed, cast an oblique glance at me, and smiled his sweet, gentle smile, a smile which had an irresistible charm, forcing one to follow his words with the keenest attention.
>
> "Does it bore you to listen to my dreams? I love talking about this . . ."

Rereading this opening, I saw how much more I was learning about Chekhov than just what he had said. I saw his animation, his cough, his sideways look at Gorky, his smile. I saw an amused self-consciousness surface for a moment, then disappear in the urgent flow of his conviction. Chekhov had been forced to finally acknowledge his tuberculosis when he was thirty-seven, after his lungs gushed blood. In proposing a sanatorium for teachers battling the disease, he showed a concern not just for teachers, but for his fellow patients. (Yalta, with its warm climate, drew many people with tuberculosis, and after Chekhov moved there, other patients often sought his help in finding lodging and treatment in the area.)

Gorky goes on to record Chekhov's long outburst about the tsarist state's urgent need to nurture teachers with better education and better pay—an outburst that spans almost two pages in the small, red-bound volume translated by Ivy Litvinov. Soon enough, though, Chekhov once again became aware that he might be boring his listener. He mocked himself for being as long-winded as a radical newspaper article; then, returning to the moment, he offered to reward his visitor's patience with tea. As Gorky observes:

> This was often the way with him. At one moment he would be talking with warmth, gravity and sincerity, and the next he would be smiling at himself and his own words. And beneath this gentle, sorrowful smile could be felt the subtle skepticism of a man who knew the value of words and the value of dreams. As well as this, there was a shade of his attractive modesty, his intuitive delicacy in this laughter, too.

If Chekhov could have read that last passage, he would likely have winced, and not just from modesty, which Gorky depicts in a scene where the great elder Tolstoy lavishly praises Chekhov's story "The Darling," while a feverish Chekhov sits, cheeks flushed, head bent, cleaning his glasses, finally responding that there were misprints in the published pages. He might also have shaken his head at Gorky's gushing tone and that pileup of positive qualities: warmth, gravity, sincerity, subtle skepticism, attractive modesty, intuitive delicacy . . . not to mention the gentle, sorrowful smile!

I juxtapose these two passages to suggest ways of thinking about voice: ways to present other voices, and ways to cultivate your own. Separating the topic of "voice" from "person" may seem arbitrary, since so much of what we know about other people emerges from what and how they communicate. Ethnographers build texts from conversations: overheard words, directed interviews, theorists' debates. These varied voices might be reproduced through specific quoted words—recorded words, remembered words, words mediated by translation—or they might be paraphrased. An ethnographer's own voice can serve as guide and interpreter, sorting out these other voices. Or, in cases of collaboration, the ethnographer's voice might join in among others' voices. As collaborative ventures become more common, ethnographers seek the voices of the people they're writing about at every stage, from deciding themes to reviewing transcripts and arranging a final form.

Gorky brought skills honed as a fiction writer, playwright, and journalist to his vivid portrayal of what Chekhov said, and how. I could see why Gorky would choose to highlight those statements that most resonated with his own idealistic revolutionary sympathies. I wondered: might Gorky have unintentionally made Chekhov a mouthpiece for his own thinking on the deplorable condition of teachers? Would Chekhov have carried on at that length using just those words? Without notes, without recordings, without the speaker's chance to intervene, one can only trust a writer's memory and gift for verisimilitude in reproducing quoted words.

Perhaps Gorky convinces us that this really *is* what Chekhov said because when he shifts into his own voice, the tone is so noticeably different. Gorky understandably writes with an elegiac affection; his friend had died, after all. But I couldn't help remembering how, in his first letter responding to the younger writer, Chekhov had enthusiastically praised Gorky's writing while also advising him to show restraint in descriptions and emotions: "You're like a spectator in a theatre who voices his delight so unrestrainedly that it prevents both himself and others from listening." Less than a year later, Chekhov offered "another piece of advice: when you're reading proofs, strike out, wherever possible, words qualifying nouns and verbs. You have so many qualifying words that the reader's attention becomes confused and wearied."

Chekhov had pointed out two essential aspects of Gorky's voice that surfaced again in the short paragraph I last quoted: the declarations of pleasure and admiration that overlay descriptions, the unabashed use of qualifying words. But in making critical suggestions, Chekhov also implied that a writer's distinctive voice could be consciously modulated, trained, improved. While I begin this chapter with ways to represent other people's voices, then, I end with strategies for cultivating your own.

How Voices Sound

Think for a moment of all that's transmitted when you hear a person's voice. Just the timbre and texture of a voice extends some sense of a personality and a mood. Here again is an example from Paul Auster, as he tries to recall his father's voice in the weeks after his father died:

> The way he spoke: as if making a great effort to rise up out of his solitude, as if his voice were rusty, had lost the habit of speaking. He always hemmed and hawed a lot, cleared his throat, seemed to sputter in mid-sentence. You felt, very definitely, that he was uncomfortable.

Notice how Auster connects the textures of outer sounds to inferred inner states. Now listen within yourself to the voice of a person you'd like to represent, not so much for words as for the overall sense of the person or a mood their speech conveys.

▹ Describe a person's distinctive voice, starting with "The way s/he spoke [or speaks] . . ." Include such aspects as timbre, vocal inflections, rhythms, characteristic pauses, gestures, and the feeling stirred in you as you listen.

How did Chekhov speak? Gorky mentions his "deep, gentle, hushed voice," Nemirovich-Danchenko describes "a low bass with a deep metallic ring," and Madame Lilin, an actress of the Moscow Art Theatre, reminds us of his appeal with women by recalling his "caressing baritone." Some also mention his laughter. Olga Knipper describes how he loved listening to funny stories, and "leaning his head on his hand and plucking at his little beard, he would burst into such hearty laughter that I would often stop listening to the narrator to follow the story merely by watching Chekhov's face." Constantin Stanislavski describes visiting Chekhov as he was correcting proofs for an edition of his collected short stories, and notices how, as he met his characters again, "he laughed good-humouredly and his rich baritone voice would fill the whole apartment."

Mostly, these contemporaries don't need to mention the self-evident: that they are all mostly speaking Russian. Nemirovich-Danchenko describes Chekhov's diction as "genuinely Russian, with a hint of purely Great Russian turns of phrase, the intonation flexible, even sometimes slightly musical, but without the slightest sentimentality." To fully "hear" this description, one would need to know the sounds of the Russian language and to understand how speaking styles marked social groups in that now distant historical time.

To describe how a language sounds is a huge challenge. But here is how the ethnographer Thomas Belmonte describes voice among the urban poor in Naples:

> In Neapolitan the voice is thick and husky and low. It makes women sound mannish. It streams outward, rough and fast, a veritable rapids of speech. Playing within it is a music, a faraway languorous water music. In even the simplest cry and certainly the commonest, the oft-repeated, "Guagliu', vien' 'a ccà" (Boy, come here), there is a complex orchestration of jubilation and longing and grief. For the call begins with an impulsive glad outburst of sound. It falls midway into a plea. It fades and dies in a low grieving moan.

Belmonte evokes the timbre of a generalized voice and its gendered association, the flow of speech and the emotions this conjures.

▹ Characterize the sound of a certain language, dialect, or accent, starting with "In ______ the voice is . . ." What associations of class or region do those sounds carry? If you were to compare this to flowing water, how would you describe the movement of sounds?

If the people you are working with speak multiple languages, try describing how their voices—and very likely their personas—shift when they move between languages. Or consider how you experience the change in voice as *you* move between languages.

Key Words, Key Concepts

Belmonte describes "Boy, come here" as the most commonly repeated phrase in Naples. Key words or phrases are a gateway not just into the recurring sounds of a language but into the values of a group or subgroup and a particular historical moment. Here is a passage from Tom Wolfe's book *The Electric Kool-Aid Acid Test*, centered on Ken Kesey and his Merry Pranksters:

> *Thing* was the major abstract word in Haight-Ashbury. It could mean *any*thing, isms, life styles, habits, leanings, causes, sexual organs; *thing* and *freak; freak* referred to styles and obsessions, as in "Stewart Brand is an Indian freak" or "the zodiac—that's her freak," or just to heads in costume. It wasn't a negative word. Anyway, just a couple of weeks before, the heads had held their first big "be-in" in Golden Gate Park, at the foot of the hill leading up into Haight-Ashbury, in mock observance of the day LSD became illegal in California. This was a gathering of all the tribes, all the communal groups. All the freaks came and did their thing. A head named Michael Bowen started it, and thousands of them piled in, in high costume, ringing bells, chanting, dancing ecstatically, blowing their minds one way and another and making their favorite satiric gestures to the cops, handing them flowers, burying the bastids in tender fruity petals of love. Oh christ, Tom, the thing was fantastic, a freaking mind-blower.

Discovering this passage, I savored Wolfe's impish movement from explication to mimicry. By zeroing in on the ethos of words like "thing" and "freak," and then showing just what it meant for freaks to do their thing at a "be-in," Wolfe flows into a great psychedelic wash of hippie language to show what being a hippie in San Francisco in the late 1960s was like.

▹ Point to a key word used by people themselves to describe what it is they do. Start with "______ was a major word in ______." Describe the social setting of the word, and quote at least one person using it. If the word has multiple or shifting meanings, try to capture its various senses and consider how it shapes or is shaped by context.

Ethnographers have long focused on language to understand how people conceptualize and categorize their lived realities. People's key words are crucial, even as they are mediated by translation and explication. But presenting these words leads one into a thicket of decisions. Should key concepts or distinctive ways of speaking be quoted consistently in the original language, so becoming part of the vocabulary of the reader? Or is it better to introduce a word once in the original, with a translated gloss used thereafter? If so, is a glossary necessary? In the dissertation that became my first book, *Storytellers,*

Saints, and Scoundrels, I often included Hindi words and phrases in parentheses to clarify my translations of folktales. I wanted to give a sense of the storytelling holy man Swamiji's idiosyncratic way of speaking, and I wanted a reader who knew Hindi to be able to judge his words on their own terms. But A. K. Ramanujan—brilliant linguist, translator, poet, folklorist—gently took me to task for being "too anthropological." He diagnosed the scattering of words in the original language as a nervous tic among anthropologists, and one that could detract from the aesthetic fullness of a translated text. I listened, half-pleased that I'd proved at least one of my points—that I could sound like an anthropologist!—but half-embarrassed that my translations seemed clunky to a literary connoisseur. Ramanujan was the person who suggested that I bring together my friend Urmila Devi Sood's corpus of folktales in a book, and in *Mondays on the Dark Night of the Moon* I used fewer parenthetical asides with Pahari words. But recurring words, like "*Bas*"—literally "enough"—with which she habitually punctuated her stories, seemed important to include, part of the flavor of her speaking style. In one draft of the manuscript, I used "Enough," but later I went back to "*Bas*," as a subtle reminder to readers of the Pahari original underlying my translation.

In ethnography, people's voices can often be grouped together, their particularity flattened in the service of establishing a general cultural pattern: "The Trobrianders say . . ." and so on. But when *particular* voices share interpretations and explications, we gain a sense of the process of conversation through which an ethnographer gained cultural knowledge. At the same time, holding to other's voices can be gift for the writing process. Sometimes, struggling to begin a book, an essay, or a grant proposal, I've rummaged through field notes; when I find someone's voice speaking on the issue I hope to write on too, I begin with a quote. If I particularly liked that person, their words offer company, helping me through the uneasy first steps of writing. Also, I'm reminding readers from the start that others—not just me—care about these issues.

▹ Locate a quote from another person on the issue you're writing about and experiment with working just a line or two into an introduction

Nancy Scheper-Hughes's *Death without Weeping* takes readers into the harsh world of the urban poor in Northeast Brazil. She unflinchingly reminds us of the huge cost of scarcity and death on people's lives, looking in particular at child mortality and mothers' attachment to their infants. Here is a section in which women in an activist group explain what they perceive as the difference between the affliction of *fome*, or hunger, and a condition known as *nervos*, "an explanation for tiredness, weakness, irritability, the shakes, headaches, angers and resentments, grief, parasitic infections . . . and hunger." Scheper-Hughes had initiated this conversation, pointing out that "a lot of what is called *nervos* looks like hunger to me. It's the *nervosness* of hunger":

> The women laughed and shook their head. "No, you're confused," they offered. "*Nervos* is one thing, and *fome* is another." Beatrice tried to explain: "*Fome* is like this: a person arrives at *feira* almost crazy, with a stomachache, shaking and nervous, and then she sees spots and bright lights in front of her eyes and hears a buzzing in her ears. The next thing she faints from hunger. *Nervos* is something else. It comes from weakness or from worries and perturbations in the head. You can't sleep, your heart pounds, your hands begin to shake and then your legs. You can have a headache. Finally, your legs get soft. They can't hold you up anymore, and so you fall over; you pass out."
>
> "And the weakness, where does that come from?"
>
> "That's because we are just like that, poor and weak."
>
> "And hungry?"
>
> "Yes, we are hungry, too . . . and sick."
>
> "So weakness, hunger, and *nervos* are sometimes the same thing?"
>
> "No, they are very different."
>
> "You'll have to explain it better then."
>
> Irene rushed in to rescue Beatrice: "*Fome* starts in your belly, and it rises up to your head and makes you dizzy and disoriented, without balance. If you eat something, you feel better right away. The trembling stops. *Nervos* begins in your head, and it can travel anywhere in the body—to your heart or to your liver or to our legs."

Notice how Scheper-Hughes includes her own probing analytic voice, pushing the women who speak with her to elaborate and specify. Notice too how in this short section, even as Scheper-Hughes clearly indicates who is speaking, she never uses the verb "said." The conversation moves on with the women offering more explanatory comments, and the chapter continues with many shattering examples of *nervos* as a social illness that accompanies chronic hunger. Scheper-Hughes concludes that "*nervos* is a somewhat inchoate, oblique but nonetheless critical reflection by the poor on their bodies and on the work that has sapped their force and their vitality."

▹ **Present an extended conversation in which people explain a concept to you. Include your questions in the dialogue.**

The selection from Scheper-Hughes is in a vivid prose form. Ethnographers seeking to reproduce voices have also experimented with forms that more closely resemble transcripts, plays, or poems.

Transcribing Conversation and Performance

We reconstruct conversations in multiple ways: from the ring of words lodged in memory, from notes taken during or after the event, and from recordings, which may seem at first to deliver the words most comprehensively and accurately. Combining these techniques can supplement the weaknesses in each form: memory and notes can add context and unspoken content—gestures, audiences, surrounding events—while recordings add precision. But transcription is yet another challenge!

For every hour of recorded words, I allow, at minimum, four hours for transcription. Should every pause, misdirected beginning, interruption, and hesitation—"umm," "like," "you know," and "yeah," "like," "you know?" again—be included? Linguists and sociolinguists might want to preserve minute details of conversations for analysis. But if your main concern is the content of what's being said, reproducing the messiness of everyday speech may only distract your readers; you might instead make some general statement about the style of speaking and then edit out unnecessary clutter. Whatever you do, explain somewhere the choices you made, and why. In a work that relies on lengthy transcriptions—and translations—your note of explanation might line up a short segment of text exactly as transcribed in the original language; a literal translation, complete with pauses and repetitions; and the eventual, smoother translation.

Kevin Dwyer's *Moroccan Dialogues: Anthropology in Question* lays out methodological, theoretical, and ethical issues associated with presenting the words of others in their fullness, rather than in fragmented extracts; in sequence, rather than chopped up and rearranged; and as evoked through guiding questions, not independent of the interviewer's presence. The very nature of the research endeavor gives power to the researcher, who defines the topic of interest, the course of interaction, and the eventual outcome. Dwyer shows how presenting the dialogues within which knowledge was mutually created throws light on this inequality. Doing so also makes an interviewer answerable for her or his guiding questions, whether insightful, insensitive, or misguided. By observing the flow of dialogue rather than being presented with summarized conclusions, readers too become actively involved in making sense of the materials.

Dwyer's book presents eleven dialogues with his friend the Faqir Muhammad in a Moroccan village in 1975. Each dialogue was sparked by an event, which Dwyer also describes. The transcript is coded typographically, with the SUBJECT set in full caps, Dwyer's ***lead questions*** in boldface italics, and his *subsidiary comments or questions* in regular italics. All the Faqir's answers are in regular type. Here is a segment from the final dialogue before Dwyer left the village that summer:

> THOUGHTS ABOUT MY ACTIONS . . .
>
> ***Could you explain to me what you think I'm doing here?***
>
> My thoughts about that are what you've told me yourself, that's what I've put in my thoughts. What you write down is what you understand, and you try to understand a lot, so that you make the others understand, those whom you teach. That is as far as my thoughts go.
>
> *Well, I ask you about a lot of things.* ***To your mind, what is the most important subject that we talk about? You know, for some subjects you might say to yourself, "What is the sense of talking for so long about such a thing?" Or, on the other hand, you might think, "Oh, that's really interesting."***
>
> As for me, I know that I'm not concerned with a single one of your questions. I know that these questions serve your purposes, not mine. I think about the questions, whether they are small questions or large ones and I think about them because they serve your purposes, not mine.
>
> *Well, what do you like me to ask you about?*
>
> It doesn't matter to me, you could even ask me about snakes.

Here as elsewhere, the patient Faqir makes clear that he's humoring Dwyer. He reminds all interviewers of the extent to which questions serve our own purposes.

▹ Transcribe a conversation you initiated, varying the type to distinguish your main questions and subsidiary questions, and the answers.

Alternatively, you could try out a more theatrical form. (And here, it's interesting to learn that Chekhov often urged other writers to try their hand at plays.) Susan Seizer opens her book on gender and marginalization in a form of drama in Tamil Nadu, South India, with a playlike representation of a conversation with male actors about gender:

> *Time*: A late morning in March 1993.
>
> *Characters in order of appearance*: Susan Seizer, an American anthropologist, in her early thirties; P. S. Nagaraja Bhagavattar, a respected Special Drama actor, in his mid-seventies; Vaiyur Gopal, his friend, another wonderful actor, in his early sixties.
>
> *Scene*: The front room of Mr. Bhagavattar's modest bungalow in Ot takadai (beside Elephant Mountain, on the outskirts of Madura) in Tamilnadu, South India. The participants sit cross-legged on a cement floor. The day is hot, and the doors are left open. Mr. Bhagavattar's wife moves in and out of the room intermittently throughout the conversation, as she is cooking in the adjacent small kitchen. Several neighborhood children have parked themselves near the open front door and stand there staring at the listener.

Seizer explains in a note that the conversation was in Tamil, that words spoken in English are in italics, that // stands for an interruption, and that bracketed numbers indicate the length, in seconds, of a pause.

> SUSAN SEIZER: You said something earlier that interests me. You said, "Men and women may be equal, but it will be the end of Tamil *culture*." Is that what you said?
>
> NAGARAJA BHAGAVATTAR: Yes.
>
> SS: But somehow, keeping Tamil *culture, we must find a way*! There must be a way for women and men to be equal, and yet at the same time for Tamil culture to survive.
>
> NB: No, no! This *equality* has already come, *nowadays*.
>
> SS: Has it?

NB: Oh yes, it has come, in the *offices* they *work* together. Everyone together, *male* and *female* are working together //

VAIYUR GOPAL: That is *foreign*. That is what is meant by *foreign* //

NB: Yes, *foreign* //

VG: This is indeed *foreign* culture.

SS: [agitated] Let there be Tamil *culture*, let Tamil *culture* remain! But let us just change this one thing in it

[1.0]

VG: *Equal* may have already come, but anyway *gents* will never give up their place.

The conversation continues, but this extract should give you a sense of how ideas central to a project can be presented through voices in conversation.

▹ **Identify a conversation key to your project. Try representing this as a play. (Or, if you can think of a different performance form favored by the people you are writing about, try out that form.)**

When people are performing in a verbal genre with an artistry intended to keep an audience engaged, it's all the more important to show the full force of emphases, gestures, dramatic pauses. Working with Zuni and Mayan materials, Dennis Tedlock has pioneered ways to transcribe spoken language so that the aesthetic form of words and performance are communicated. In Tedlock's method every pause produces a line break, spaces between letters indicate slowing down, boldface signals loudness (and smaller type, reduced volume), and pauses longer than a second and a half are marked by strophe breaks with arrows.

Here is an example from Tedlock's *Breath on the Mirror.* On a mountaintop in the company of three ethnographers, the modern priest-shaman Don Mateo offered a distinctive Mayan version of how Adam and Eve were made. Tedlock (referred to in the text as don Dionisio) transcribed this from a tape, translating from Quiché and Spanish. The story itself is indented, with the narrative of its telling—which includes descriptions of gestures, other audience members, and Tedlock's explanatory asides—extending to the left margin. This excerpt comes after Eve has been made from Adam's rib as he slept. Waking up, Adam "s l o w l y" comprehends her presence and starts to run away, **yelling**!

> He s a w **then** that the woman was seated there,
> he was startled, he started to run away from fright.
> And then
> "N o o o, Adam, no, Adam, haven't you heard?
> Jesus Christ left me with you
> I'm your companion."
> **"Y i i i i h!**
> Get yourself unglued from me,
> get further away," yet she was two cords away . . .

a cord is a measurement native to these mountains, roughly twenty yards,

> . . . some
> two cords or some
> twenty yards,
> or twenty
> I don't know what.

"He was frightened," says don Dionisio, and don Mateo replies,

He was frightened.
"A A A
dam! dam! dam! Sit down man, Jesus Christ left me with you, I'm your companion, I'm your companion."

▹ **Transcribe a segment of narration using Tedlock's transcription style. Read this aloud to see what you need to add. Now ask another person to read from your transcription. What else might you need to add?**

These three examples are reminders of the many different ways of trying to capture in print voices that have been fixed by recording devices. It's up to you to choose—or improvise on—which form best suits your own project and sensibilities. Consider conferring with the people you're writing about for their insights on form. Whenever possible, share drafts with the original speakers so they might share the same luxury of refining their spoken words that you enjoy when polishing your writing.

Quotation and Paraphrase

Reproducing every word of the conversations weaving around us is clearly not feasible—or even interesting. When is paraphrase more efficient? When are direct quotes indispensable? When does specifying who said what and when advance the cause of ethnography as possible testimony—as in the case of land rights cases involving indigenous people? When might presenting verbatim quotations expose a person or a group to embarrassment or even danger? Again, these are questions to be thought through afresh with every project.

Among anthropologists, the genre of life history is most devoted to reproducing other people's actual words. In this form too, anthropologists usually adapt and transmute a person's spoken (or sometimes written) words by editing, rearranging, contextualizing. Some stretches of words are quoted; others are summarized. Describing how she transformed the Mexican peddler Esperanza's life story for publication. Ruth Behar reminds us of the literary artistry that must be exercised if fieldwork materials are to be assembled into a comprehensible and compelling story:

> As I undid necklaces of words and restrung them, as I dressed up hours of rambling talk in elegant sentences and paragraphs of prose, as I snipped at the flow of talk, stopping it sometimes for dramatic emphasis long before it had really stopped, I no longer knew where I stood on the border between fiction and nonfiction.

Even before the anthropologist's aesthetic choices come into play, storytellers' own aesthetics and cultural conventions will have strongly shaped how their experience is narrated. Behar shows how the themes of rage, suffering, and redemption inform Esperanza's narratives, and organizes her presentation of Esperanza's life, her own life, and her interpretive commentary around these themes. Similarly, in working to record the life of the Mexican American curandera Eva Castellanoz, Joanne Mulcahy was so struck by Eva's use of metaphor in healing practices that metaphor came to direct her own writing choices. In *Remedios*, each chapter of the unfolding life story opens with Eva's metaphorical expression of a difficulty and its suggested remedy.

In *The Life and Hard Times of a Korean Shaman*, Laurel Kendall introduces us to a woman shaman, "Yongsu's Mother," who through her life had transmuted disappointments into good stories for other women, and Kendall became one in a long string of temporary audiences for the shaman; as she acknowledges, "Yongsu's Mother's tales were already more than twice told when first I heard them, and they would continue to be told long after I left the field." Here's an example of how Kendall mixes quotes and summaries when recounting how she and her field assistant approached Yongsu's Mother for a survey:

> She fielded our queries with an air of amusement, prompting my assistant to giggling self-parody.
>
> "Do you practice birth control?"
>
> "Am I a chicken? Can I lay eggs without a mate?"
>
> And so we continued. Her stepson, aged nineteen, now there was a worry! He had given up studying so she bought him a cow to raise, but then his elder sister (that bitch) lured him away to work for her instead. Yongsu's Mother, stuck with the cow, sold it at a loss. She was still smarting from this most recent evidence of her stepchildren's ingratitude. Her recollections of her own family tapped an older betrayal. Her father had died when he was shot by an invisible supernatural arrow (*kunung sal*) at a funeral feast. She didn't miss him at all, though, or even want to think about him, because he had taken a concubine and given his own children grief.

Notice how this selection includes just one line of direct quotation. That line, however, introduces Yongsu's Mother's feisty tone, which Kendall then carries through the entire summary of the conversation.

▹ Describe a conversation, mixing memorable quotes and inflecting your summary of what the person said with the tone in which they said it. Or select from a series of conversations, with one bright thread of exchange pulled to the foreground for direct quotation.

Here is a section from Paul Stoller and Cheryl Olkes's *In Sorcery's Shadow*, a memoir of Stoller's apprenticeship as a sorcerer in Niger:

> Towards the end of my survey, I interviewed a shopkeeper named Abdou Kano, a short hunchbacked man with an infectious, toothless smile. Abdou told me, among aother things, that he spoke four languages (Songhay, Hausa, Fulan, and Tamesheq). My work with Abdou completed, I walked next door to inteview Mahamane Boulla, who, like Abdou, was a shopkeeper. I asked him how many languages he spoke:

"Oh, I speak three languages: Songhay, Hausa and Fulan."

During our conversations about languages, Mahamane asked me how many languages Abdou spoke.

"Abdou says he speaks four languages."

"Hah! I know for a fact that Abdou speaks only two languages."

"What! Is that true? How could he lie to me!" I stood up abruptly. Red in the face, I stormed back to Abdou's shop. Abdou smiled and greeted me.

"Ah, Monsieur Paul. What would you like to buy today?"

"Abdou, Mahmane has just told me that you speak only two languages. Is it true?"

"Yes, it is true. I speak only two languages."

"Why did you tell me you speak four languages?"

Abdou shrugged his shoulders and smiled. "What difference does it make?" He looked skyward for a moment. "Tell me, Monsieur Paul, how many languages did Mahamane tell you that he spoke?"

"Mahamane told me that he speaks three languages."

"Hah! I know for a fact that Mahamane speaks only one language. He can speak Songhay and that is all."

"What!"

I stomped back to Mahamane's shop.

"Abdou tells me that you speak only one language. But you just told me that you speak three languages. What is the truth?"

"Ah, Monsieur Paul, Abdou is telling the truth."

"But how could you lie to me?"

"What difference does it make, Monsieur Paul?"

This exchange crackles with energy partly because of its swift forward flow. If every word in these larger conversations had been painstakingly presented, we'd miss out on the comic timing of this story. Sometimes, being an effective storyteller requires quoting only the parts of conversations that matter to an unfolding story.

▹ Reconstruct the thread of a topic you learned about through conversations with different people and include your own reactions.

Pauses, Guarded Words, Words in Veiled Forms

Ethnographers can easily become attached to what's explicitly spoken, what's formally explained. But what of the power of pacing, pauses, and the unspoken? A skillfully selective writer can evoke more from what's left tantalizingly unstated and implied than what's actually said. To return again to Chekhov: the celebrated actor and director Constantin Stanislavski, who cofounded the Moscow Art Theatre, recalls how in his plays Chekhov "often expressed his thought not in speeches but in pauses or between the lines or in replies consisting of a single word." Stanislavski elaborates on Chekhov's revisions during the first production of *The Three Sisters*. In an early draft, the character Andrei had a two-page monologue describing a wife. Then Chekhov wrote from Yalta with corrections:

> Then suddenly came the order to strike out the entire monologue and in its place put these five words, nothing more:
>
> "A wife is a wife!"
>
> If you think about it carefully you will find that this short phrase contains all that was said in the two pages of monologue. That was very characteristic of Chekhov: what he wrote was always succinct and compact. Each word of his was accompanied by a whole scale of varying moods and thought. He did not state them explicitly but they came to your mind of their own accord.

Cultural conventions may also demand that certain ways of speaking be avoided. Among the Eveny of Siberia—traditionally nomadic reindeer herders on the taiga who were forced by Soviet colonization to organize themselves into collective farms—a high premium is placed on emotional restraint in speaking. In *The Reindeer People*, Piers Vitebsky observes:

> I had heard many warnings against the casual splashing around of words, as well as of projecting them too forcefully, from stories of people who had offended the taiga by speaking or singing loudly, to the loss of respect accorded to Russians, and later Americans, when television arrived in the village and they saw characters in dramas shouting at their families. Sharp, unguarded words could take on a force of their own and even kill, like a curse.

Having paraphrased the general chorus of warnings, Vitebsky harnesses the power of a particular story retold in a person's actual words:

> Someone in the village once told me, 'I had a long-running battle with one of the Farm bosses, and one day I heard of a new plot he was hatching against me. I was so angry that I said out loud, "Why

> isn't that old bastard dead yet?" Even at the time, I had a bad feeling about those words. Well, exactly a year later that boss was at death's door and he sent for his son, who'd been my childhood friend. The son was due to go herding that day, but he stayed close to his father. It turned out that the father was too tough to die and the same night his son died instead. His son had taken on the impact of my words.'

Notice that Vitebsky attributes this story only to "someone in the village." This example points not only to cultural forces but to political hierarchies, for this is not just any man being spoken against but a boss in a Soviet-backed reindeer farm. In accounts of lives set in repressive states, publishing exact words of critique can reveal political positions and endanger speakers. An ethnographer's challenge then becomes how to express these positions while also protecting particular individuals. The anonymity of the storyteller can be preserved through vague attribution, general glosses, or consciously altering identifying details. Conversely, state power may promote accounts by official representatives that highlight self-justifying words. An ethnographer might draw on such words while also subtly showing—through descriptions and juxtapositions—the hypocrisy of the speaker or of the position taken.

▹ How might cultural and political constraints modulate the voices you're working with? Illustrate what's considered best left unsaid with an example of a speaker's overstepping the usual limits.

Feelings and subjects that are considered inappropriate in direct conversation can sometimes be revealed through alternate forms of expression. Living with a Bedouin community in Egypt, Lila Abu-Lughod found that principles of honor and modesty made it inappropriate for people to reveal feelings of vulnerability. Yet when "veiled" in sung poems called *ghinnawa*, such feelings could be expressed without compromising honor or modesty. She describes Mabruka, a middle-aged woman whose husband had just married a younger second wife. He had stayed longer than usual on his honeymoon, then returned to Mabruka, bringing some groceries but not everything that the household needed. Then he left again:

> He took his gun to go hunting, and as he walked away, she commented to me, "It's been ages [literally, years] since we saw him." I asked sympathetically if she missed him. She replied abruptly, "No

way. Do you think he is dear to me? I don't even ask about him. He can come and go as he pleases."

Moments later she recited a few poems. One suggested her consternation over the events of the recent past, brought up by his sudden appearance; another conveys a sense of betrayal:

They always left me
Stuffed with false promises . . .

dīmā khallō l-'agl
'āmrāt bimwā'īdhum . . .

In the course of this interchange Mabruka's mother-in-law and a close woman-friend joined us. They spontaneously added to her poems, voicing what they assumed she was experiencing. These same women had previously scolded her, or teased her, for her angry reactions, but through poetry they consoled her by showing their emphatic concern.

Abu-Lughod goes on to quote these painful poems sung in solidarity by the other women. By presenting the *ghinnawa* poems in Arabic, she allows readers to appreciate the aesthetic compactness of these poems in the original as well as through translation. Recourse to poetry allowed these older Bedouin women self-expression without their having to state a position in direct conversation. Indeed, people often couch their feelings within genres of expression that point to a shared "tradition"—proverbs, jokes, parables, folktales—thus ducking personal responsibility.

▹ If the people you're writing about commonly consider certain feelings and topics to be unspeakable, describe an occasion in which they actually expressed their thoughts about these topics.

Also consider listing some of the forms in which you write or hope to write. What does each form constrain or make possible to say? What audiences might each potentially reach? Knowing this can help develop the range of your own voice and chosen forms of expression.

Cultivating Your Own Voice

"Voice" doesn't just refer to spoken words; it also implies the sense of a communicating presence behind written words. Without even using "I" or explicitly introducing the self, the choice, sequence, and rhythm of words establishes a witnessing, evaluating presence.

Largely because of voice, some writing magnetically commands attention—you can't help but keep reading. Other writing can seem about as appealing as a half-swallowed mumble, a mechanical recitation, an incantation of prestige-laden names and terms.

Chekhov once observed, "There are big dogs and little dogs, but little dogs must not fret over the existence of the big ones. Everyone is obligated to howl in the voice that the Lord God has given him." Chekhov was offering encouragement to another writer, Ivan Bunin, to continue writing even though others—like Maupassant, whose fiction Chekhov greatly admired—had already displayed dazzling talent. (Chekhov also urged Bunin to write every day, and to take a professional attitude to writing; Bunin went on to become the first Russian to receive the Nobel Prize for Literature.)

This idea of "howling" in an innate voice may suggest a belief that a writer has just one voice; but then too, all the critical and supportive letters Chekhov sent to fellow writers about their work surely indicate hope that one's howling can improve. As the writer Tanya Schepkina-Kupernik (who at one point shared her lover, the beautiful actress Lidia Iavorskaia, with Chekhov) remembered, "He had the ability to feel interest in and deep inner sympathy with the literary efforts of others." The advice he gave her included "Love your heroes but never say so aloud!" and "Abandon 'ready-made phrases' and clichés."

Occasionally I meet a person—usually a woman—who tells me that she's lost her voice. It's not that she can't write at all, she says. Depending on her age, she might have successfully written term papers, reports, a dissertation, even a book or two ... But it doesn't feel like her voice, she says. Rather she's writing in a way that she once learned was safe, and after a while she couldn't remember other ways with words. She welcomes exercises of the sort I suggest, but still, she confesses, it feels risky to share unguarded writing. As our conversation continues, I usually learn that once, long ago, she wrote a journal, or poems, or stories. She would love to write again in her own voice, with her whole self, but for now ... it's too scary.

Fear squashes a voice. Professional training narrows the color and range of possible tones. Too many outer demands brick up a flowing voice, forcing it so far underground you may forget its sounds. How then is it possible to remain true to yourself as a writer while also attending to all the complications of a life involving other people's expectations and demands? How can you keep your own voice while gaining the training for a livelihood and meeting the ongoing challenges of keeping a job?

As I began reflecting on how to write about voice, I wondered if professionally trained singers might have insights to offer. I remembered Sheila Dhar, who was both a Hindustani classical singer and a vibrantly appealing writer. I treasure her book *Raga'n Josh: Stories from a Musical Life* not just for what I learned about Hindustani music and musicians, but also for her warmly sympathetic voice. In her introduction, Dhar explains how for years she had been telling and retelling certain stories to friends because "wonderful things become even more wonderful for me if I can share them and dreadful things more bearable." Her friends urged her to write down these stories, and in doing so, she learned that "unrolling the pictures in my mind through the written word felt exactly like singing. At any rate it took me to the very place I occupy in my head and heart when I try to express my whole self through the idiom of music." As she explains:

> For me the act of singing ideally means recognizing and intensifying my own identity, and communicating it in the rigorous traditional idiom of an ancient musical language. This ideal is not always achieved, but when it is, my musical utterance inalienably carries within it the flavour of everything that has ever happened to me, and of all the emotional landscapes I have traversed. The feel of my grandfather's beard, the smell of the dank basement in our childhood home, the aroma of my Ustad's cooking . . .

This evocative paragraph continues, foreshadowing many moments that will be elaborated on in future chapters. By linking her musical voice and her writing voice, Dhar offers what I see as three potential steps for developing one's voice: first, finding ways to recognize the self; second, intensifying this recognition through attentive practice; and third, gathering knowledge, skill, and versatility in the chosen idiom.

So how might a writer go about this? To recognize the self, one needs to set aside time to turn inward. One of Dhar's teachers, the flamboyant Pandit Pran Nath, insisted that "you have first to listen to your own breath and then to the self it embodies." While students of other teachers in Delhi were sailing forward, learning ragas and compositions, Pandit Pran Nath insisted that Dhar first find her own voice by singing just one note—the shadaja, or *sā*—during traditional early morning practice. She quotes his instruction:

> Take the note and with your breath draw a line of sound on the silence. Think of it as a pencil of light. If it wavers and warps, discard it and start another. You have to do this all your life, for many hours every day, until you can draw a perfect line of sound. Slowly the line will gain body in your perception and seem to you to be a broad band with a middle and sides. The ... practice will help you to stay in the dead center, and this means being in tune. A tone is not a point but a melodic area to be explored.

I read and reread that passage, thinking of that perfect line of sound as an opened flow of communication. Only dedicated practice, intensifying the recognition of self, allows a line to expand into an "area to be explored." The Hindustani classical singer's solitary exploration of sound reminds me of writers' building routines that protect needed time from outside demands. Every writer works out her or his own form of practice, something I will elaborate on in my postscript, "Writing to Be Alive." The practice that has helped me is trying—not always successfully—to fill at least one handwritten page in a notebook each morning. This page could be about anything at all, and is above all a way to be with myself. I find that this solitary, inward-turning writing practice helps me sort through thoughts, images, feelings, stories. Finding words for the fluctuating welter of each day's inner themes can grant me a more limber and confident voice for writing that faces outward, as a performance for others.

The regular practice of writing, and also reading and listening, speaking and performing, helps develop a versatile voice. Dhar is a wonderful storyteller as well as performer. In her own narration, she chooses pitch-perfect words; quoting others, she captures intonations and mannerisms precisely, to the point of parodying individuals as well regional Indian accents. As a singer too, she could be a wicked mimic. One of her choicest musical impressions was of the sort of primly off-tune performance that a new bride from her own Kayastha community might embark on when trying to show off musical skill (a performance that the great Begum Akhtar commandeered in order to convince another legendary singer, Ustad Fayyaz Khan, to take on Dhar as a disciple—and he was indeed persuaded by this ability to willfully sing out of tune!)

▹ Choose the distinctive voice of a writer you've become familiar with through your project. (This need not be someone you admire.) Choose a passage that you feel is characteristic, with distinctive turns of phrase and rhythms of language. Now rephrase what you think the person is trying to say, using your own words and voice. Reflect on the difference.

I direct anyone who might have selected a jargon-laden passage to the sociologist C. Wright Mills's impish presentation of a selection from one of the prestigious scholarly books of his time, Talcott Parsons's *The Social System*. In his own book, *The Sociological Imagination*, Mills devotes a chapter to "Grand Theory," with Parsons as his primary example. After each dense, almost impossibly ponderous and abstruse passage from Parsons, Mills begins, *"Or in other words,"* and clearly, concisely summarizes.

Chekhov's trail led me to Vladimir Nabokov's *Lectures in Russian Literature*, first delivered to college and university students in the United States in the 1940s and 1950s. Nabokov follows Russian writers who represent the heyday of Russian literature, from the mid-nineteenth century to the first decade of the twentieth—a period that roughly matches the span of Chekhov's life (1860–1904). As a native Russian speaker and emigrant Russian writer from a later time, Nabokov brings sumptuous insight to his readings of six writers, starting with Gogol and ending with none other than Chekhov's friend Gorky. Setting the historical stage for these writers, Nabokov contrasts the oppressive Soviet dictum that writing must celebrate the state with the space that earlier writers in tsarist Russia had negotiated between a government that did not allow criticism and radical critics who demanded a social message.

A writer is always vulnerable to political circumstances, whether consciously or unconsciously, willingly or unwillingly. As I've mentioned earlier, Chekhov's stories, plays, and nonfiction all had to pass before tsarist censors who could demand revisions, forcing him to delete or alter passages, and simultaneously, radical critics who would complain that his complex characters and indeterminate endings didn't take a clear enough political stand.

Moving from state strictures to institutional settings, I also reflected on issues of voice in academia. Graduate students cultivating a distinctive voice must be savvy to the orientations of committee members; tenure-track faculty must keep a watchful eye on what's considered necessary and appropriate for a tenure dossier; academics submitting work for publications must become attuned to the tone of particular journals or presses. Professional survival and success can depend on learning to strategically pitch a voice to a setting, even as it remains your own. At the same time, ventures into alternative creative spaces that allow more experimentation with one's full expressive range—without fears for livelihood—can, I believe, deepen and enrich a professional voice.

Nabokov remarks how Chekhov used everyday, "word-in-the-street" Russian, and yet "managed to convey an impression of artistic beauty far surpassing that of many writers who thought they knew what rich beautiful prose was." Here is Nabokov's miraculous passage describing his perception of Chekhov's accomplishment:

> By keeping all his words in the same dim light and of the exact tint of gray, a tint between the color of an old fence and that of an old cloud. The variety of his moods, the flicker of his charming wit, the deeply artistic economy of characterization, the vivid detail, and the fade-out of human life—all the peculiar Chekhovian features—are enhanced by being suffused and surrounded by a faintly iridescent verbal haziness.

This passage opens out startling ways to think of "voice": through words, light, color, sensibility. Nabokov lingers over the artistry in "The Lady with the Little Dog," then moves from that particular story to summarize seven "typical features" of Chekhov's stories more generally. The first feature is "The story is told in the most natural way possible . . . in the way one person relates to another the most important things in his life, slowly and yet without a break, in a slightly subdued voice." Nabokov's appreciation of Chekhov suggests a prompt:

▹ Choose a writer you admire and try to describe the magic of her or his voice, starting with "I admire ______'s voice." Consider the kinds of words the writer uses and characterize the voice through metaphor, evoking color, light, music, landscape, weather, or the kind of interaction this writing makes you imagine.

Articulating what draws you toward the singular voice of a writer opens out another way to consciously develop your own voice. Becoming aware of the marvelous range of writers' voices is an inspiration for finding the pitch, tone, and rhythms that most grant you a sense of inhabiting yourself as you write.

* • * • * • * • * • * • * • * • * • * • * • * • * • * • * • * • * • * • *

VOICE

Present a dialogue that reveals information or insights central to your project. (This could draw from interactions you participated in, overheard, or are piecing together from others' accounts.) Pay attention to the textures, cadences, and intonations of voices, including your own. 2 pages.

FIVE Self

In April 2010, a dream allowed me to talk to Chekhov.

I had dialed Chekhov from one of several scattered cottages on a Kangra tea estate. Stepping aside from a sociable group, I had entered a small room to hold an old-fashioned black telephone receiver against my ear. A table lamp glowed over a comfortable sofa, a low table, oil paintings of landscapes.

"Listen!" I excitedly told Chekhov, "I've found two stories . . ." Both were his; the first I mentioned by name and the second I outlined by plot. I offered to read the second story to him over the phone.

Chekhov was gracious. I sensed his listening presence accepting my exuberance with what seemed almost like resignation. But just as I was about to start reading the story aloud, the line went dead. I set down the receiver and returned to my husband Ken and the house party. Beyond a screened porch, crickets whirred. Moths flitted between lamps.

"It's so hard to get a good connection to nineteenth-century Russia!" I clucked.

Quickly, while Chekhov was still available, I opened my laptop to see if I might Skype him. With this chance to rethink my impulsive call, I realized that I hadn't calculated long-distance phone rates. Reading him an entire short story would surely be more sensible over Skype. But would Chekhov have a Skype account? Yes! I found an address along with a thumbnail image of him, cheek in hand, musing from behind a desk.

I prepared to try the Skype connection and instead woke up.

Chekhov's image lingered in the Wisconsin morning. I sorted through details from the dream again, wishing I could reenter that space more thoughtfully. Why had I so boisterously carried on about reading aloud his writing, setting the conversation on my terms? What might he have said if I'd paused to properly listen? What was the dream telling me? Reaching about for coordinates in the present, I recalled that I was still sketching ideas for chapters 4 and 5, "Voice" and "Self." I wrote out the dream and retold it to Ken. (Having tolerated my Chekhov fixation for some months, he was amused and goaded me to entertain friends with the lead: "Did you hear about Kirin Skyping Chekhov?")

I'm still thinking through the mysterious texture of associations that the dream wove together. A tea estate in the Himalayan foothills was most likely the closest to a Russian country estate that my unconscious could muster. I'd recreated a summer house party of the sort that might have taken place at Melikhovo, the home in the countryside near Moscow that Chekhov was able to buy for himself and his family in 1892. The landscape paintings were like those by Chekhov's friend Isaac Levitan that Chekhov hung in his study. "Listen!" was how Chekhov appears to have begun many of his own conversations. (Some translations say, "Look here!") In my enthusiasm to tell him about his own stories, I had been mimicking him.

I wondered where I might have glimpsed that image on Skype. I began searching my study, dismantling vertiginous stacks of books about Chekhov. I found the photograph on the cover of Rosamund Bartlett's edition of his selected letters. Looking again at the young man at his desk, facing the camera but apparently lost in thought, I wondered if this image offered a glimpse into the creative trances that Chekhov's mother and sister had described. The photograph is from 1891—the year after his journey to Sakhalin. The connection to a book of letters reminded me of how Chekhov can seem so present in his correspondence, even as he clowns around with different personas. (While he signs off mostly as "Yours, A. Chekhov," he also plays with variations like Antonio, Antoine, and Anthony, absurdities like Schiller Shakespearovich Goethe, and even the name of a brand of a laxative mineral water.)

Bartlett's edition is distinctive in translating the complete and uncensored versions of some letters that were made available only a hundred years after Chekhov died. As she observes in her introduction, "In some respects, Chekhov's letters are the autobiography he never wrote." When Chekhov was asked for personal accounts, he claimed to suffer from "autobiographophobia": "Being forced to read, let alone write, any details about myself is the purest torture." But he occasionally complied with short—very short, and sometimes absurd—summaries, with a few facts and mentions of his dual allegiance to medicine and literature. An entry in his notebook advises against collecting details of a writer's life: "When I see books," Chekhov writes, "I am not concerned with how the authors loved or played cards; I see only their marvelous works."

How much, in your writing, do you want to let on about what you dreamed and how you "loved or played cards"? Would you prefer to remain an indistinct presence? Are you willing to draw yourself into the light as a recognizable figure, an avatar who takes on a sort of demarcated life and goes out to meet others on your behalf? Just which aspects of yourself are you ready to share? These questions provoke strong opinions! People have different levels of comfort in revealing themselves. Then too, depending on the genre you have chosen and the audience you're writing for, you will contend with very different expectations of what's appropriate.

Readers are prepared in advance for a writer's extended presence on the page if the writing is labeled as involving the self—as a memoir, following some thread of experience (for example, fieldwork, illness, family, career), or as an autobiography, taking on the larger span of a life. Additionally, "auto-ethnography"—ethnography of one's self or one's group—is growing in popularity in the same disciplinary circles that favor ethnography. The term claims various genealogies. Auto-ethnography dissolves notions of ethnography as dependent on encounters across cultural difference, instead turning a descriptive and analytic eye on one's own experience as shaped by larger structures and processes—including the professional background of academia. However, not all scholars who write about aspects of their lives that spill beyond formally defined fieldwork choose to label their work as auto-ethnography.

In the great tangle of possible story lines connecting you to the materials you're writing about, think hard: which threads might enhance a reader's appreciation of textures and patterns within the materials you're weaving? What do readers *really* need to know about you—which aspects of your background or your present situation? How much self-revelation is, in the slang of the times, TMI—Too Much Information?

Life brings us many powerful experiences and insights; not all need to be crammed into one text or even one kind of text. You could write an ethnography and then revisit the experience in an auto-ethnography or a memoir or a personal essay or a poem; you might equally draw on the disguises of fiction and recast the materials in a short story or a novel; you might choose another medium or invent a new form. Just because something happened to you doesn't mean that it will be interesting to others: it's your challenge to relate that experience in an interesting way. Choose your form carefully, with a sympathetic eye to readers' expectations and patience. You risk writing in ways that might not count toward advancement within a discipline or profession; simultaneously, you gain a chance to be more than a disciplined or professionalized self.

Narrating

A writer's voice necessarily implies a self with certain sensibilities, regardless of whether the first person is used. Bring in an "I" and set it rolling (like the spool it resembles), and you'll be unfurling a long thread, a thread you can then use to artfully stitch together diverse experiences and insights.

Rather than slamming down a list of intersecting coordinates about who you are (gender, race, class, ethnicity, sexual orientation, age, regional background, and so on), stand outside of yourself and think of how you might slip in detail only as needed, in the same way that a writer might build an interesting character. To do this, you'll need to cultivate distance. Try to move beyond the centripetal urge of being the star. Stand back: discern the ways you are linked to others by shared experiences, or interactions across differences and inequalities. Consider the possibility of different perspectives.

I found Philip Lopate's advice on turning yourself into a character in personal essays very helpful. Reflect on who you are, he suggests, with curiosity and amusement; establish your signature quirks, your humanizing contradictions and conflicts, the larger categories that have shaped who you are: "Turning oneself into a character is not self-absorbed navel gazing, but rather a potential release from narcissism. It means you have achieved sufficient distance to begin to see yourself in the round."

Here are two prompts to begin establishing yourself as a character embarked on the quest you're writing about:

▹ **Describe yourself when first engaged in your project. What most intrigued you, what did you hope, and what did you fear?**

▹ **During the same period, how do you think you appeared in the eyes of others? What categories might they have drawn on to place you?**

Whether or not you choose to make yourself into a fully complex and "round" character for readers—and not all writers want to do this—placing yourself as an experiencing presence within a text can still be a supple means for linking different moments in time and different steps in your thinking.

Among the anthropologists who wield narrative with admirable ease is Michael Jackson—ethnographer, novelist, memoirist, and poet. Here's an example from one of his books, *In Sierra Leone*, that caught my eye as I looked at my shelves seeking support for my point and a prompt for readers. In this book, Jackson describes returning in 2002, toward the end of a brutal civil war, at the express invitation of his friend Sewa Bockarie Maraha, or "S.B." S.B. had known Jackson since his earlier fieldwork, in 1969, and now asked for his help on an autobiography. Noah, S.B.'s younger brother, had been Jackson's field assistant, and his nephew was called "small S.B." Here is a scene soon after Jackson's arrival in Lumley:

> It was almost dusk when I left Noah, and small S.B. drove me back to my hotel. The tide was out, and as we approached the Aberdeen ferry bridge, I asked small S. B. to slow down so that I could look for S. B.'s old house on the edge of the inlet. Another casualty of the war, it stood in ruins near a grove of huge mango trees. Out on the mudflats, women and children were searching for shellfish, and I remembered an evening, long ago, sitting on the balcony and looking at this

> very scene, when Rose told me that it was from here that the slave ships set sail for the Americas with their human cargoes. At that moment, small S. B. broke into my thoughts, telling me that scores of rebel soldiers were brought to the bridge in January 1999, summarily shot, and their bodies thrown into the bay.
>
> As the bluish twilight settled over the mangroves, the mudflats, and the sinuous channels of water beneath us, I found myself thinking how easily scenes of horror and tranquility succeed each other on the same stage, and recalled Marlowe's words in *Heart of Darkness*, as he and his companions watched the light fading on the sea-reach of the Thames: "And this also has been one of the dark places of the earth."

Notice how, by including himself, Jackson moves his account through space and time. With phrases like "I remembered," "I found myself thinking," and "I recalled" he also starts to complicate the scene with layers of history, emotion, and literary allusion. Situating his descriptions in his own witnessing sensibility, he allows us to better imagine the pain of revisiting a place marked by extreme violence.

▹ Situate yourself in a scene and describe the thoughts that opened around the moment: a memory of your own, recollections of a historical event, a general insight, or connections to a related piece of writing.

Explaining

"So, what are you working on?"

This question flies at us again and again, an existential inquisition. How do you vary your answer for those who know hardly anything about your materials, and those who are already knowledgeable insiders? What sorts of response cause listeners to light up, giving you the full focus of intrigued attention? Through the years, I've found that paying attention to how I sum up a project, looping bright ribbons around it, can teach me something about the weight, shape, and hue of the materials. The stories and the summaries I choose in conversation sometimes find their way into the writing itself.

Your most engaging spoken words can help shape spaces of orientation—a title, preface, or introduction. In addition to borrowing and adapting these spoken words, you might also experiment with *showing* yourself telling others about what you're doing, and depicting their responses.

Zora Neale Hurston—ethnographer, novelist, short story writer, memoirist, playwright—deftly embeds metacommentary on her project in the opening pages of *Mules and Men*. After a short preface by her teacher, Franz Boas, her own introductory words set her interests in ironic counterpoint to disciplinary authority: "I was glad when somebody told me, 'you may go and collect Negro folk-lore.'" That person, she implies, is the influential Boas himself. Hurston introduces her project of returning to her hometown to gather folklore from several angles: by quoting the words she used to justify the plan to Boas, by describing her own inner reasoning on why it made sense to return to a familiar place after she'd been changed, by spelling out what she *didn't* return for (to be admired as a daughter returning from the north with a college degree and a car), and finally by stating the reason she *did* choose to go to Eatonville, Florida—because rich folklore materials could be reliably and safely found here.

Hurston's first chapter opens with her arrival in Eatonville. The arrival scene is common to many ethnographies; here it is also a reunion. When Hurston drives into town, she sees a group of men assembled over a game of cards on a store porch. She calls out greetings as she stops the car. The men at first don't seem to recognize her, but then B. Moseley exclaims, "Well, if it ain't Zora Hurston!" and they come out to welcome her. By showing them asking how long she will stay, and with whom, Hurston is also letting readers in on her general research plan and establishing her familiarity. The exchange continues with the arrival of the mayor.

> "Hello, heart-string." Mayor Hiram Lester yelled as he hurried up the street. "We heard all about you up north. You back home for good, I hope."
>
> "Nope, Ah come to collect some old stories and tales and Ah know y'all know a plenty of 'em and that's why Ah headed straight for home."
>
> "What you mean, Zora, them big old lies we tell when we're jus' sittin' around here on the old store porch doin' nothin'?" asked B. Moseley.
>
> "Yeah, those same ones about Ole Massa, and colored folks in heaven, and—oh, y'all know the kind I mean."
>
> "Aaw shucks," exclaimed George Thomas doubtfully. "Zora, don't you come here and tell de biggest lie first thing. Who you reckon want to read all them old-time tales about Brer Rabbit and Brer Bear?"

"Plenty of people, George. They are a lot more valuable than you might think. We want to set them down before it's too late."

"Too late for what?"

"Before everybody forgets all of 'em."

"No danger of that. That's all some people is good for—set 'round and lie and murder groceries."

"Ah know one right now," Calvin Daniels announced cheerfully. "It's a tale 'bout John and de frog."

Notice how Hurston introduces local views on her project through this exchange. Showing herself arguing that plenty of people are interested in stories and want to collect them before they disappear, she seems to be mischievously echoing Boas's own project of salvaging remnants of vanishing cultural forms. But she then immediately subverts this concern by quoting the men's assurances that there's no danger to the tradition of storytelling.

▹ Write a scene that shows you explaining your project to the people you'll be writing about; to a respected authority figure; or in conversation with yourself.

Evoking

Any project evokes prior experience. The pull of your past will be especially strong if your project is taking you home. But also contrasts posed by a very different place can evoke both familiar and hidden memories.

In his genre-crossing book *In an Antique Land: History in the Guise of a Traveler's Tale,* Amitav Ghosh combines his skills as an ethnographer, historian, essayist, and fiction writer to depict connections forged—and divided—across space and time. Ghosh takes readers on two entwined research journeys, through the past and in the present. His trail leads through documents and archives as he seeks to discover more about a mysterious twelfth-century Indian slave of a Jewish merchant who traded between Egypt and India. Simultaneously, as an Indian student studying social anthropology at Oxford he is doing field research in Egyptian villagers.

A running line of humor is generated by depictions of how Egyptian peasants reacted with curiosity and astonishment to him as a young foreigner from India. At one point, Ghosh is interrogated by a group of men who have assembled for the wedding of the brother of Ghosh's friend Nabeel. Nabeel is an agricultural student who in an earlier chapter has displayed a moving empathy for Ghosh's distance from home.

At the wedding, middle-aged male visitors sitting together in a guest room want to know what Ghosh is doing there and how he learned Arabic, and as usual they want to hear about life in India. Ghosh tries to escape to watch the wedding festivities, but as the evening wears on, he's called back to talk more with the curious men. They sit together companionably, smoking cigarettes and coal-burning shusha pipes, and ask Ghosh all kinds of questions about Indian culture and customs: what happens to the dead? what guides people's behavior? do women undergo clitoridectomy? are boys circumcised or "purified"? The questions turn to the issue of Ghosh's own "purification," and he is unable to respond:

> I looked at the eyes around me, alternately curious and horrified, and I knew that I would not be able to answer. My limbs seemed to have passed beyond my volition as I rose from the divan, knocking over my shusha. I pushed my way out, and before anyone could react, I was past the crowd, walking quickly back to my room.
>
> I was almost there, when I heard footsteps close behind me. It was Nabeel, looking puzzled and a little out of breath.
>
> "What happened?" he said. "Why did you leave so suddenly?"
>
> I kept walking for I could think of no answer.
>
> "They were only asking question," he said, "just like you do: they didn't mean any harm. Why do you let this talk of cows and burning and circumcision worry you so much? These are just customs; it's natural that people should be curious. These are not things to be upset about."

The almost anthropological curiosity of the Egyptian villagers has evoked a gut reaction in Ghosh, a strong impulse to escape. But why? His friend Nabeel is bewildered, and the chapter ends with Nabeel's reassuring words. The next chapter begins with a detour into Ghosh's own background:

> I sometimes wished I had told Nabeel a story.
>
> When I was a child we lived in a place that was destined to fall out of the world's atlas like a page ripped in the press: it was East Pakistan, which, after its creation in 1947, survived only a bare twenty-

> five years before becoming a new nation, Bangladesh. No one regretted its passing; if it still possess a life in my memory it is largely by accident, because my father happened to be seconded to the Indian diplomatic mission in Dhaka when I was about six years old.

Ghosh goes on to recall his childhood memories of communal riots in Dhaka, and of crowds of Hindus periodically taking shelter in the walled garden of the diplomatic compound. He recalls memories of an occasion when a large crowd of men carrying torches surrounded the garden, memories that as he says are out of synch, "like a sloppily edited film," and eerily stripped of sound.

Ghosh's parents' Muslim friends called the police, who dispersed the mob. Year later, reading old newspapers, Ghosh learned that as that riot was erupting in Dhaka, a parallel riot had raged in Calcutta, with Muslims attacked by Hindus, and with stories of Hindus intervening. Ghosh points out the centrality of symbols in communal riots, and "men dismembered for the state of their foreskins."

But in the Egyptian village, Ghosh felt unable to explain much of this background to Nabeel or anyone else. He points to the different historical experiences of India and Egypt, and writes, "I could not have expected them to understand an Indian's terror of symbols." Examining such moments of strong reaction, then, throws light not only on oneself but also on the gaps between self and other.

▹ **Describe a moment of interaction to which you responded strongly. Try to excavate the grounds for your response, including images lodged in your memory. Then stand back to reflect on how this might relate to larger shared experiences.**

Placing himself and his memories amid these interactions in Egypt, Ghosh also illuminates one of the larger themes in his book: the legacies of the past in the present. Turning to Ghosh's wonderful novel *The Shadow Lines* (1989), written a few years before this nonfiction book, one recognizes a recreation of the same twinned riot in Calcutta and Dhaka from the perspective of another young schoolboy. The same event, it seems, was retold in different genres and stories.

Transforming

Going about daily life in the company of others, as both participant and observer, grants insights at many levels, from the "materials" to be written down to less tangible bodily knowledge; in the process, a person is transformed. Ernestine McHugh's *Love and Honor in the Himalayas: Coming to Know Another Culture* is an unusual fieldwork memoir based partly on notes that she diligently kept as a college undergraduate inspired by Gregory Bateson. Arriving in a remote Gurung village in the Himalayan foothills of Nepal in the 1970s, Ernestine was adopted by kind and charismatic Lalita, or Ama. She lived with Ama's family for almost two years, and went on to write a BA honors thesis. Later, after more fieldwork, she wrote a dissertation too. In this memoir, McHugh uses origami-like skill to fold the perspectives gained through her further training into the story of her younger self.

As a malleable young woman eager to fit in, Ernestine had been energetically socialized by her honorary family and others in the Gurung village. She was instructed in their language, how to wear their clothes, how to do their everyday work. She recalls how her body changed through her association with the local architecture, the steep mountain paths, the practice of carrying heavy loads for long distances:

> In Gurung villages, doorways are low, so you have to bow a little as you enter a house. The beds and mats are hard; you cannot sink into them. People's bodies are contained, arms and legs held close to the trunk, so that large untidy gestures seem out of place. My body changes in Nepal. As I stayed there, my center of balance shifted lower. This made me more stable going up and down trails and helped me move more effectively in a lungi or sari. I also became more erect. Carrying loads strapped to my head strengthened me, and when a bundle of grass or a pot of water was removed, I felt my whole body rise upward, so light I could float.

▹ Describe how you have been transformed by your project, starting with "My body changes in . . ." and situating your account in social practices. Move from there to any other changes to aspects of yourself.

Carrying a heavy load stands at the center of a conflict with Ernestine's adoptive father, the headman Jimwal, or Apa. All dressed up with red ribbons in her hair and Ama's gold bangles on her wrists, Ernestine had joined the family on an outing by foot across the mountains to visit relatives. She was being presented as an honorary daughter and had been tutored in advance on the appropriate kinship terms to use with those they would meet. Relatives in a distant village gave Apa the special gift of a package of deer meat, and as they set off on the return journey, Apa asked Ernestine to carry this heavy, bloody, and smelly package for a while. After a few hot hours of walking, they rested, and then Apa handed Ernestine the pack again. He assured her it would be just a little longer, but she ended up carrying it all day. The next morning, as another set of relatives looked on, Apa once again gave her the pack. Feeling tricked and bullied, Ernestine strapped on the pack and set off, reaching the village home first. She threw the pack on the floor, burst into tears, and told those left behind that Apa had made her carry the deer meat all that distance. Then she stormed off down the mountain slope to spend the night somewhere else.

A day later, her anger cooled. Ernestine returned to find Apa weaving outside the house; he asked whether she'd eaten and suggested that she go inside, where she was fed. "This is not at all like your country, is it?" Ama asked when they had a moment alone. After telling Ernestine that Apa was hurt and upset that Ernestine got angry and ran off, Ama acknowledged that she understood why Ernestine felt mistreated: of course no one would want to carry a big, stinky pack of deer meat. She then stepped back from the particulars to spell out an underlying cultural logic: that children should carry loads for the honor of the elders in a household. "It doesn't look good for an important man like your father to carry a pack while a big daughter walks along free," Ama said, and she went on to explain:

> From the time our children are small, we coax them. We might say, "Now Seyli, just carry this as far as the resting place." So she agrees and picks it up. But at the resting place we say, "just a little farther," like that, on and on until we are home. . . . Children here know from the time they are young that it's all a fake; they make all kinds of excuses not to pick up a pack because they know they won't get to put it down again. Now Apa was just treating you like a real daughter, but you couldn't understand that because people don't do it that way in your country.

Looking back at how Ama patiently laid out these assumptions, McHugh writes, "She had been able to compare her world to mine and find the emotional slippage, and with her explanation she created a platform for me to stand on and see the differences."

If not for the misunderstanding, though, Ama might not have spoken out so clearly. The emotional pain of misunderstanding can bring something that's been taken for granted into clearer focus. Recalling moments of conflict is a powerful narrative and analytic tool.

▹ **Recount a painful miscommunication. Who helped you understand what was going on?**

Reframing

Shahram Khosravi's *"Illegal" Traveller: An Auto-Ethnography of Borders* is a powerful example of how life experience that was never intended to be fieldwork can be the source of anthropological understanding, connecting an ethnographer to theories and to the experiences of others subjected to the same structural forces. Khosravi was born in Iran, with roots in the once-nomadic Bakhtiari tribe (featured in the early ethnographic film *Grass*). Finishing high school in 1986, during the war between Iran and Iraq, he, like many young men of his generation, faced conscription. Knowing that his chances of surviving the war were slim, his family urged him to leave Iran. He made arrangements with a human smuggler to cross the border into Afghanistan. The smuggler, though, turned out to be in cahoots with the police, and Khosravi was arrested, interrogated, and jailed. After a month he was released on bail and returned to his family. A few months later, working from a contact made through a cellmate, he sought help in crossing from Homayoun, a young Afghani man who had been living in Iran as a construction worker.

Saying goodbye once more, Khosravi did not know whether he would see his family again. He took in their tranquility of the neighborhood at dawn, imagining the morning routines that would soon be repeated: children leaving for school, parents leaving for work, the family's elderly woman neighbor leaving for the market, their Jewish family doctor leaving for his clinic. In contrast, Khosravi knew his own departure was a powerful turning point.

> After two decades, memory of that morning still evokes enormous pain. I kissed my 12-year-old sister in her sleep. I preferred not to see her tears, which would have torn me apart. My father stayed in his room. The unbearable grief of separation paralyzed him, making him unable to perform the farewell ceremony. My sister told me later that he did not come out of the room for two days. He did not eat, and did not talk. Through the window, they saw him sitting on the chair, bent forward and staring downward. I heard later from my sister that he

> blamed himself. He, the 'big man', the bear hunter, a man from whom many, even strangers, sought protection, could not protect his own son. My brother, who would take me to the airport, was waiting in the car. In my mother's embrace, the outside world, war, migration, borders, future and past all ceased to exist. I breathed her smell, the smell of my childhood, probably the first smell I experienced in my life, until she took a step backward and muttered something like 'Go!' My older sister poured water behind me when I crossed the threshold, an Iranian ritual expressing hope that the traveller shall come back soon. I did not turn back, did not look back. I could not. But in the car, I could no longer keep my eyes away from my mother. She stood at the door, not crying so as not to discourage me. But she was shaking. I knew that a storm was wracking every cell in her heart, as it was doing in mine. When my brother put the car in gear, I could not breathe any more and my tears poured out. Since then they have not ceased to run.

In his short book, Khosravi turns the intensity of such sorrow inside out, making it a source of connection to the many other people whose lives have been torn apart and even destroyed by borders: not just the policed borders between nation-states, but also the internal divisions within societies.

▹ Recall a turning point that has forever marked your life. Describe that moment. Consider the social forces at work and also describe others whose experience connects to your own.

Through great hardship and uncertainty, Khosravi was able to cross through Afghanistant into Pakistan, from there into India, and finally on to Sweden, where he became labeled a refugee and eventually trained as a social anthropologist. Through his book, Khosravi continually situates stories from his personal experience and his research materials within the frames of larger theories of borders, border transgressors, migration, citizenship, and human rights. Even as he draws on theories to illuminate his experiences, then, he also uses experience to interrogate theories.

▹ Make a list of theories that your most powerful experience might connect to.

Do you choose to unpack these theories, or will you leave them implicitly enacted, for others to identify if they choose? As I see it, that's one of the primary differences between calling a work auto-ethnography—which by definition claims a more analytic, specialized reader—and calling it memoir, which might potentially reach a wider audience of nonspecialists. As Khosravi points out, by bearing witness to injustice, his book also shares an affinity with the genre of *testimonio* associated with Latin American life stories from the marginalized and dispossessed.

Connecting

Chekhov's active Skype account in my dream suggested his ongoing ability to communicate through twenty-first-century technologies. January 29, 2010, marked 150 years since his birth, with many publications and celebrations honoring the occasion. His plays are still performed, his stories and letters still read, his stories now adapted into films. Allusions to Chekhov, and the adjective "Chekhovian," are sprinkled across discussions of literature and blurbs on book covers, regularly anointing authors who write with some semblance of his compactness, compassion, indirection, and minute detail.

I found Richard Peavear and Larissa Volokhonsky's new translation of Chekhov's stories in an airport bookstore in 2009, keeping company with assorted best-sellers. A passage from one of the shortest pieces in the collection leapt out at me, as though speaking to my own project. The story is called "The Student" and was first published in April 1894. Chekhov told friends that this was his own favorite of his many stories. Like many of his other stories, it tells of the telling of a story.

A seminary student is returning home along a deserted path on a Good Friday evening. At first the spring weather is lovely: blackbirds are singing, and from the swamp he hears something that "hooted plaintively, as if blowing into an empty bottle." But the weather turns wintry, and he is cold. Since cooking is prohibited that day, he is also hungry. He wretchedly walks along, reflecting that the same wind had blown in the past, along with "the same savage poverty and hunger; the same leaky thatched roofs, ignorance and anguish, the same surrounding emptiness and darkness, the sense of oppression." These miseries, he thinks, will stretch even a thousand years forward. "And he did not want to go home."

The student sees a fire in the distance, an outdoor fire in the gardens of two peasant women, a mother and daughter who are both widows and who greet him as he nears. He joins them and, warming his hands at the flames, muses aloud that the apostle Peter had also sought such warmth on a cold night, long ago. The student goes on to tell the story of Peter, who had stood by a fire alongside servants of the high priest as Jesus was being interrogated and beaten. At three different times, Peter was asked if he knew Jesus, and he said he didn't. Then toward daybreak, he recalled how, a few hours earlier at the Last Supper, when he had pledged to follow Jesus no matter what, Jesus had countered that Peter would deny knowing him three times before the rooster crowed. Remembering, Peter left the courtyard to weep. "I picture it," the student says, "a very, very silent and dark garden, and, barely heard in the silence, a muffled sobbing . . ."

Finishing his retelling, the student sees that the two women are visibly moved; the older woman is crying and her daughter looks stunned. When he continues on into the windy night, his hands are once again cold. Looking back, he can still see the fire. He reflects that if the women were so moved, then what he had told them had a relation to the present: "If the old woman wept it was not because he was able to tell it movingly, but because Peter was close to her and she was interested with her whole being in what had happened in Peter's soul":

> And joy suddenly stirred in his soul, and he even stopped for a moment to catch his breath. The past, he thought, is connected with the present in an unbroken chain of events flowing one out of the other. And it seemed to him that he had just seen both ends of that chain: he touched one end, and the other moved.

As the student—who Chekhov observes in an affectionate aside is just twenty-two—continues toward his home, he thinks of how truth and beauty guide life even in places of sorrow; truth and beauty, he feels, will continue to guide life into the distant future. Displacing that dull sense of meaninglessness and oppression is a feeling of well-being and expansive happiness.

▹ **Describe an interaction that opened out a feeling of connection beyond yourself.**

This story resonated with my own interest in oral storytelling, even though I wasn't familiar with the biblical narrative. I noticed how the student's ability to sympathetically reimagine faraway events on a Good Friday evening in the Russian countryside fanned a known story so it burned brighter. His retelling moved his listeners and altered his own perspective. Selves met other selves through the medium of storytelling, and all were transformed. I also reflected on how, as a crucial link in the chain of retellings welding together real and imagined tellers, Chekhov's own self suffuses "The Student" without ever being clearly delineated. Though Chekhov considered himself an atheist—partly in response to his tyrannically religious father—his childhood familiarity with the rituals and stories of the Russian Orthodox Church pervades many of his stories.

Reading works by Chekhov and about Chekhov, haven't I too grasped at one end of a long chain of human transmission, tugged across time and space and language toward other selves? My retelling of "The Student" doesn't do justice to Chekhov's words as I've met them in translation. Yet in being moved myself, and struggling to express why, I've twisted another link into the chain of retellings.

▹ Write about an image associated with your project that has especially caught your imagination in thinking about the project itself.

Anton Chekhov, 1891.

In drafting this chapter, the most difficult of all to write, I've looked from time to time at the photograph that appeared in my dream:

Chekhov is not yet wearing glasses. He is just 31, still broad-faced, apparently healthy, with thick eyebrows, tousled dark hair, a beard and moustache. His left hand balances his cheek, index and middle finger raised to temple. His right hand isn't clearly visible, but the angle suggests a pen in hand. He looks into the camera but seems lost in choosing the next word. . . .

* · *

SELF

Narrate a moment of revelation or humiliation that shifted your understanding. Describe not just your own perspective, but also how others most likely perceived you. 2 pages.

POSTSCRIPT *Writing to Be Alive*

Sorrow and joy are true brothers, declares a Pahari proverb that I learned from my friend Urmilaji in the course of ethnographic work in the Himalayan foothill region of Kangra. By calling these brothers "true," the proverb emphasizes that they're bound up in the same everyday circumstances, more closely connected than cousins or even honorary kin. I sometimes think of that proverb when I'm writing—or trying to write. Like life, which writing reflects and refracts in parallel streams of words, the process of writing can drag you down or buoy you up. You can find yourself spinning, unable to move ahead. You can be stuck in the muck by the shore. In moments of grace, you might discover yourself aligned with the current, drawn forward by the words around you. Even during breaks, words and sentences will arrive, as though spoken in your mind—you'll rush to get back to the writing.

How do other writers keep moving forward, despite the ups and downs? I've found that looking to others' insights is a source of support, solace, and encouragement. Talking is helpful, as is reading what other writers have to say about the process of writing, whether through poems, articles, essays, memoirs, biographies, or books about writing.

Even someone as inspired, purposeful, and productive as Chekhov could sometimes be bored and uncertain. I was struck by his ebb and flow of confidence in a series of letters he wrote Suvorin in the summer of 1891—perhaps while sitting at one of the desks from my Skype dream. In May, from a small summer cottage he'd rented along with his parents and siblings, he wrote:

> On Mondays, Tuesdays and Wednesdays I work at my Sakhalin book, and the other days, except Sundays, at my novel. On Sundays I write little stories. I'm enjoying working, but alas! my family is large, and when I'm writing it's rather like being a crayfish in a cage with other crayfish: a little crowded.

Bright, expansive, Chekhov was writing in three genres simultaneously. When the family found a larger place to rent—an old house on an overgrown estate, with room for guests—Chekhov set up a new routine that allowed him to continue with this outpouring of creative activity. As his biographer Donald Rayfield reports, "He rose at 4.00 a.m., made coffee and worked while the household slept until eleven. Then they walked, played, lunched, gathered mushrooms, caught fish and rested. Anton sat down to work again at three and worked until dark at 9.00 p.m., after which came supper, cards, bonfires, charades, arguments, personal and philosophical, and visits to neighbors." But in August, writing the book on Sakhalin, Chekhov complained to Suvorin, "I am bored, I am bored." "There are times," he confessed, "when I long to sit over it from three to five years, and work at it furiously; but at times, in moments of doubt, I could spit on it." (A few years later, in an even more startling image of a moment of distance from writing, he quipped to the writer Lydia Avilova that the literary scene was so oppressive that "when I write nowadays or think of how I *have* to write, I feel such a sense of revulsion as if I were eating cabbage soup from which a cockroach has been removed, if you'll pardon the comparison.")

Do all these moods sound familiar? Energetic engagement alternating with severe self-doubt unfortunately seems to be part of the process of writing. At least this is my experience. The only way to learn whether the cycles of misery and elation are making for good writing is to keep going.

Working with Words

Here are some general tools for writing. You'll find most these—and more—in just about any good book on writing (a list of such books heads the references). But just as good tools work best when used again and again, it seems that we can be regularly reminded of ways to enliven writing.

- Honor the range and flexibility of language. Choose your words with care and precision and make every word count. Keep a thesaurus at hand; the versions available online can be handy, but to visit with extended families of related words and think through all the possible inflections of meaning, I prefer the printed pages of *Roget's Thesaurus*.
- Attend to verbs. Watch out for the passive voice. You can locate passive constructions by looking out for the auxiliary verb "to be" and all its permutations in tense, and verbs that act on subjects. Use the passive voice selectively, when you want to convey the ways in which the world seems set, still, fixed, with people stranded in situations and operated on by forces beyond their control. When people themselves are acting—exercising agency, pondering strategy, pursuing tactics—switch to the active voice. When you spot the passive voice in your own writing, ask yourself who or what is the source of the action. If you can discern the subject, and can visualize some movement it makes or causes, find a strong verb to capture that motion.
- Sentences are easily overburdened. Weighed down with too many clauses and disparate images, they groan and grow weak. Distribute the weight by splitting unwieldy sentences. Some writers can make their long sentences into works of great beauty, but even they do so selectively.
- Recognize also that sentences thrive on variety. Make an effort to vary their rhythm and length.
- Paragraphs too can be overburdened. Pages with no breathing room can suffocate readers. I try to include at least two or three paragraphs on a page.
- Be kind to your reader! Readers are busy people. Their attention

is a gift. Think of the times you've been irritated by another person's seeming carelessness with your own time and energy when you've tried to puzzle through their writing; step out of your own preoccupations to imagine the hardships you could cause a potential reader. Why should they bother?

- Read your writing aloud when you can, or at least read slowly enough to take in every word. You quickly learn where the words are wrong and the rhythms don't work.
- Don't make readers hunt for the antecedents to your pronouns! Vaguely gesturing toward what came before can be a chronic problem in academic prose.
- As you're editing drafts, continually ask yourself if there's anything you could prune away. You might need to print out what you've written to gain a sense of its general shape. Cut out sections that draw energy away from your central intent, and plant them in a different file, where they still might grow. Consider each word in a sentence, and trim off anything unnecessary—words don't mind, they will be used again in other situations. Sometimes, abundant words are necessary, but choose each one consciously.

The Writing Process

Anthropologists are experts on theories of ritual. For writers too, rituals can help summon inspiration: by marking a transition into a state of concentration; by demarcating a stretch of time separate from other obligations; by fostering solidarity; by alleviating anxiety. In my classes and ethnographic writing workshops I sometimes invite each person to tell us what her or his rituals might be. As we go around the room, it soon becomes clear that what works for one person can seem amusingly eccentric to someone else. I also invite you to reflect on your own writing rituals. If a particular chair, pen, font, sweatshirt, food, café table, kind of music, or anything else grants you a feeling of well-being and open connection to yourself, build on this knowledge to help you write.

My own writing is helped by first stilling my mind, quieting down all the nervous chatter in an attempt to clear space in which new ideas and images might arrive. I work best in the early morning, before the day's expectations have come hammering at my sense of self. If I don't sit to write in the early morning I can wander in a fog through the rest of the day—doing other things but disconnected from making something that's distinctly mine. I keep on hand a journal with smooth pages and a fountain pen. If I'm at the computer, changing the font can give clarity to what has seemed opaque. I am helped out by strong Assam tea with just the right amount of milk. Sometimes I listen to music for a sense of movement that I hope will carry into words. Sometimes I take a walk.

Curiosity sets me moving as I research a project. So too curiosity about what I'll learn through writing is a renewing source of energy. Curiosity quiets my self-doubt; writing becomes less an arena in which obstacles must be overcome and more of a space to receive whatever comes. When my curiosity seems blunted and hidden, turning to others for conversation can remind me of the pleasures of communication and discovery.

That's my own experience, at least. Here are some more general tips that I've compiled through the years by observing myself and asking others about their strategies.

GETTING STARTED

- Any time is a good time to begin. Start right now with a prompt like "What I most hope to write about is . . ." or by jotting down an image or idea.
- Write an abstract of the project, trying to synthesize and summarize your aspirations.
- Create an outline that gives intelligible shape to what you hope to write. (I think of this as a map or itinerary for a journey. You may find some other metaphor that helps you keep track of your progress.)
- If the overall form is not clear, start with the episode or idea that most energizes you and trust that that the structure will emerge from the materials.
- Some people need a talismanic first line to launch them into a project. Look through your materials and see if you might already have received that gift in something you've written or in someone else's spoken or written words.
- Write yourself a note about what you most hope to write the next day, and before going to bed, place this under your pillow. (The advice of a dear friend's grandmother.)
- If you're having trouble settling down to compose, try talking to a friend about what you're trying to write. Someone else's curiosity

and interest, or just sympathy, can remind you why the project is worthwhile. You might even ask if they would keep you company as you begin.

- Make a writing date with a friend, whether in person or from a distance. Tell each other your intentions and then, after a specified time, report back to each other.
- Go for a walk, a swim, a bike ride while the intention to begin ripens.
- Order the space you write in. Clear away papers you've put off filing, tidy up any remaining piles, sharpen pencils. Arrange flowers. Light candles. Do whatever will make the space seem welcoming to your muse.

MOVING FORWARD

- Designate a stretch of time every day when you will outwardly and inwardly disconnect from external demands. This might be in your own home or elsewhere: an office, a café, a library, a bench in a garden.
- Unplug. Turn off and hide your phone so there is no way that it can grab your attention. Turn off the wireless connections on a computer. Seductive little distractions will burrow into your time and send your mind spinning in multiple other directions.
- Plug into a specially selected playlist of music that helps you write. My students have reported working to world music in an unfamiliar language so they won't fixate on lyrics, to soothing instruments, and to heavy metal. (In the days of cassette tapes, I wrote much of my dissertation to the rousing reggae beats of Bob Marley.) At least one student has reported that dancing to his favorite music helps words arrive.
- What else galvanizes you? An anthropologist friend tells me that she goes out and walks until she can feel the rhythm of the words that she'll write in her stride. (She lives in a place without snow and ice.) A person in a workshop shared with us that she needed to see nature in movement for words to flow. A student confessed that he loved showers and would take several on productive days. Another friend praises the selection of small, interesting objects on his desk: between sentences he might handle and admire a rock, a shell, an intricately carved bead.

- Find spaces where you can be still but your mind can roam. When I was a driven undergraduate, my writing teacher, Grace Paley, once gave our class the assignment to go lie under a tree. The tangle of branches against the sky proved very inspiring.
- Turn to alternate forms of creativity. I find that anything that involves selecting and combining ingredients can help me write, especially cooking and beading projects. Several students have mentioned baking (adding that housemates, friends, and colleagues tend to appreciate these outbursts of creativity). One student reported that she brought out a sewing machine to make patchwork collages.
- Treat writing time like a job, where you put in a certain number of hours, whether or not you're inspired.
- Periodically consult yourself on what it is that *you* most want to say, even if the project's terms are set from outside (an assignment, a thesis, a book contract, whatever.)
- Similarly, when you're feeling intimidated by the weight of what others have already written, look again at your own materials. Find ballast by remembering what's distinctive about your own contribution and the supportive energy of all those who have helped you with it.
- Connect again with the people you're writing about. Their interest in your project can help remind you of why it matters. (Don't be discouraged if they aren't that interested. When I proudly brought my dissertation to Swamiji, he suggested that I place it on his altar; he didn't want to discuss what I'd written, and instead offered to teach me how to cook a certain delicious snack. Later, as I turned the dissertation into a book, Swamiji's light acceptance of whatever it was that I'd written helped lighten my own process of revision.)
- Break up the project into manageable chunks. Make lists of which segments you hope to write about on a given day.
- Pace yourself with regular breaks. But if you find yourself immersed and focused, continue writing. Concentration is precious.
- Consider rewards for small milestones (two pages? five pages? a section or chapter completed?).
- If you're stuck, allow yourself to leave gaps that you'll fill in later.
- Find a friend to write with. But make a pact that no matter how amusing a thought you may have, neither of you will break into

the other's space. The other person's absorption will hopefully encourage your own.
- Do not let larger drama—including concerns about the meaning and purpose of your writing—deflect you. Just keep writing.
- Get sleep. Whatever your writing schedule or pressing deadlines, be sure you work in enough hours for your muse to be rested.
- Remember to enjoy your larger life.

MOVING PAST WRITER'S BLOCK

- Don't despair. Finding yourself hopelessly stuck is part of the process. Fallow fields can be resting, preparing for new growth. Things will eventually shift. You just don't know when or how.
- Try to describe what you're experiencing. At a moment when I was really stuck on this project, I wrote this note: "Sometimes writing to external demands can be like trying to squeeze sweet juice from a stone. The unrelenting hard density of the project won't give way to process; the project shoots out of reach; grasping tightly, straining until muscles ache and eyes sting, you are sore, tired and sad, but still nothing yields. What happened to all that bright talk about being alive in the writing? Wouldn't it be easier to just walk away?" I found comfort in expressing myself, and the hope that even this misery might eventually bring insight.
- Reflect on why you've been pulled up short at this particular moment. Has some sprite of your own negativity grown disproportionately large, threatening to gobble your creative vision? Or are you feeling struck down by outer evaluation? If your project seems to have withered away under someone else's scrutiny, take a deep breath and try to understand that person's intention and perspective. She or he probably has a different aesthetic sense, different goals; try to understand what those might be rather than allowing this divergence to knock you down so hard that you can't stand up. Remember, frank criticism can be the highest form of respect. Putting aside your own wounded sense of being misunderstood or undervalued, look again: is there anything at all helpful you can take away from that criticism, or the experience of being criticized? (If nothing else, reflecting on how you're feeling now may later help you give criticism more constructively to others.)
- If you're writing within an institutional structure, or your liveli-

hood depends on writing, look pragmatically at the larger forces that demand that you do something in a particular way. View these outer demands and hurdles as something to engage with tactically; they are in no way an accurate indicator of your own creative worth. Your sense of yourself as a writer might benefit from allowing yourself to play simultaneously at a different project that doesn't officially "count."

- If your faith in yourself and your project is wavering badly, reach out to a friend or relative who you know believes in you and what you're trying to accomplish. Tell them what you're going through, and what you need from them (don't expect them to read your mind). Ask if they might read something for you. Resist brushing off reaffirming words: listen closely and write down any especially helpful words to reflect on later.
- Alternatively, reach out to a reliably supportive friend who is also a writer. Set up regular times to report back to each other.
- Read other writers on problems of writing. Feeling blocked is painfully isolating. Remind yourself often that many others have found themselves in the bleak spaces where you are now marooned; many others are in that space right now. Rainer Maria Rilke's *Letters to a Young Poet* has for me been a steady fount of reassurance through the years. An acupuncturist friend put a copy of Julia Cameron's *The Artist's Way* into my hands during one of my most despairing seasons of drought, and though I never made my way through Cameron's many exercises for recovering creativity, the physical presence and intent of the book was itself a comfort. Grant yourself some time to browse the interviews with well-known writers that the *Paris Review* has been recording since the 1950s—this treasure trove is now all available online at http://www.theparisreview.com/interviews.
- Revisit the tips in the "Moving forward" section. Might any of them be useful?
- Allow yourself a complete break, even a vacation of a few days. You might be working too hard and have lost perspective. Think again about your project once you feel rested and renewed.
- Look through your materials and find some small way to reengage: edit a page, transcribe an interview, line up works for your bibliography. You may find yourself reminded of what drew you to the project and once again moving forward.

REVISING

Revising is key to every step of writing. The company of other writers can help you reenter, reconsider, and further polish a piece of work. If you've shared your work with another person or with a group, here are some questions that you might ask these trusted readers about your work.

- Did the first sentence draw others forward to read?
- What do others think your piece is "really" about?
- What do they consider the most arresting moment, image, or turning point?
- Does each paragraph logically flow into the next? Did readers have any ideas on how you might you modify the order in which ideas or scenes are presented?
- Are they able to picture the people you are describing? What other senses might your piece engage?
- List three things about strong writing that *you* learned from reading others' pieces. Share praise; be encouraged.

FINISHING

- Finishing is hard. Use the galvanizing force of deadlines. If you don't have an external deadline, make a pact with someone else that you'll both finish something at the same time
- Think in terms of a procession of drafts. Following folklorists' insight that every retelling is but one version of a larger story, think of your written productions as versions too, versions that recast a story when it is told in a different voice or reshaped from a different perspective. Knowing that a multiplicity of versions is possible can alleviate some of the crushing weight of completing a first draft, and also the sting of critical comments.
- If you're working on a long project—like this book—you may be exhausted and uncertain of your perspective by the time you near the end. Yet you can't relax because you know you have a deadline. You work and work but no longer trust your own judgment or feel confident that anyone else will care. Don't lose faith in your earlier self who chose this project and in all the people who helped you along the way. Work on your acknowledgements as a way to remember others' support. If your friends can bear to hear you mop-

ing about a project that's gone on too long, turn again to them for support.

- Forgive yourself in advance, knowing that whatever you write will never be complete or perfect. You could spend the rest of your life polishing one piece of work. Do the best you can, and prepare to let it go.

Even as you come to the close of a project, reread and revise your words until you can recognize the energy of what you've been trying to express. Your words may carry some part of the times and places you've lived in, the people and voices you've known, and your own quirky sensibility toward readers—those you already know and those you may never directly meet. And there you will be, as Chekhov has been for me, alive in the writing.

Acknowledgments

"I'm writing a book about writing, and I'm stuck."

After a morning when I could no longer bear revising chapters and worked instead on a first draft of these acknowledgements, I said these words to a friend. I had run into him while out shopping, and as we caught up on news, he asked what I was writing. He met my reply with guffaws rich with goodwill. "That's a good joke!" he said.

Not so funny, I thought. All too often while writing this book I lost my sense of balance and direction. I am grateful to every kind person who helped me to my feet and who urged me forward.

I thank my students in classes and participants in the workshops on ethnographic writing and memoir writing I have taught since 1994. You are too many to name, but working with you has shaped the insights that appear on these pages. Particularly in the section on writing tips, you might find some echo of something you shared about your own writing process. Also, I thank my companions in leading some of these workshops: Joanne Mulcahy, Kathy Robinson, Helena Wulff, Ruth Behar, Nalini Natarajan, Emily Martin, Katherine McCaffrey, and Christopher Kelty.

My own teachers' words echo in my mind when I confront challenges in composition. For this boon, I particularly thank Grace Paley, Alan Dundes, and Renato Rosaldo. Renato deeply influenced my approach to writing ethnography, and his affirmation and advice helped me find the tone for this book.

Many dear friends granted me companionship along the lonely road of writing, and their presence pervades these pages. I thank them all, knowing that this book would not exist without their help. Joanne Mulcahy offered invaluable inspiration and ideas, and several days of intensive writing and conversations at the early stages of envisioning this book. Marian Goad read the first draft of every chapter, and sometimes second and third drafts too; again and again, her steadfast belief in this project, her insights into the heart of what I was trying to accomplish, and her editorial intuitions reminded me why I had begun. Frank Salomon reintroduced me to Chekhov, first suggested that I was getting so far into the Chekhov materials that I might want to consider using them throughout the book, and inspired me with his appreciation for what I discovered. Kevin Dwyer offered pitch-perfect critical comments that helped me envision this book's relation to both ethnography and to Chekhov. Peggy Yocom gave me radiant solidarity through weekly writing dates. Agate Nesaule has been a steady source of inspiration through ongoing conversations about writing and she also supportively read the complete manuscript. Maria Lepowsky once again rescued me with her generous, astute, and clearheaded reading of sections of the final manuscript when I could no longer see clearly.

I thank Anne Haggerson for her clarity, energy, and astonishing efficiency in handling the many details of assembling these pages, and Susan Rottman for thoughtful comments on the first completed draft. Tom Durkin, social science librarian extraordinaire, provided unstinting background assistance. Along the way, as I shared parts of the book, I was at different times enormously cheered by the supportive readings and insights of Peter Agree, Susan Bernstein, Julie Cruikshank, Julie D'Acci, Elizabeth Desan, Lewis Koch, Sarah Levin, Ernestine McHugh, B. Venkat Mani, Christi Merrill, Todd Michelson-Ambelang, Sidney Mintz, Hemant Shah, and Jeanne Thieme.

I am grateful to all at the University of Chicago Press who helped this manuscript emerge into its final form: Alan Thomas for encouraging the germ of an idea, David Brent for shepherding the manuscript through stages of review and sharing his perspectives on ethnography, and Laura Avey for her ready help with several key details of production. I am so glad to have worked with Joel Score as copy editor for two books: his eye for detail and sense of structure has showed me the skill and artistry of copy editing. I am also grateful for the comments of the manuscript readers, Michael Jackson and Michelle Murano.

My mother, Didi Contractor, read, commented on, and enthusiastically supported this book from its first glimmer of an idea forward. I'm grateful for her role in nurturing this book and all my writing through the years.

Ken George—cherished friend, perspicacious colleague, bemused partner—supported my writing at every stage and in ways so countless that I won't attempt to recount them. When I heard him describe this book I was wearily struggling to finish as "a how-about? manual," I was so surprised and entertained that I found a fresh momentum to wrap this up for delivery into other readers' hands.

Notes

The following notes are keyed to page numbers. Italicized phrases indicate material quoted in text. References to Anton Chekhov in citations are abbreviated AC.

ALIVE IN THE WRITING

ix–xiii For these few introductory pages alone, I could fill a large book of notes. But I will try to be concise in offering what I have found to be important orienting works.

Ethnography has been appropriated and adapted by many disciplines beyond cultural anthropology: folklore, sociology, history, geography, religious studies, educational policy, journalism, legal studies, rhetoric, cultural studies, English, creative writing—the list goes on. Much has been written on ethnography as a research method: among the books I've found useful in anthropology classrooms or which colleagues have particularly recommended are Angrosino 2007, Davies 2002, and Ellen 1984, though there are many, many more such handbooks available. Also see collections of writings about fieldwork, for example, Jackson and Ives 1996 and Robben and Sluka 2007.

Books on ethnography as a form of writing are also legion, and I won't even attempt to list articles. Among the books I've effectively used in classrooms through the years are Abu-Lughod 1993, Behar and Gordon 1995, Clifford 1988, Clifford and Marcus 1986, Dwyer 1982, Geertz 1988, Jackson 1989, Marcus 1998, Marcus and Fischer 1999, Rosaldo 1989, Stoller 1989, Van Maanen 1988, and Wolf 1992. For an illuminating set of strategies for reading ethnographies that also implicitly inspire writing, see Gay y Blasco and Wardle 2007. For recent collections of anthropologists reflecting on ethnography, adapted from presentations at American Anthropological Association annual meetings, see Sharman 2007 and Waterston and Vesperi 2009. For more on collaborative ethnography, see Lassiter 2005.

Practical strategies for generating and shaping ethnographic prose are fewer and far between. For shaping ethnographic fieldnotes, Emerson, Fretz, and Shaw 1995 is helpful. Sunstein and Chiseri-Strater 2002 combines fieldwork exercises, extracts of writing, and writing exercises for undergraduates across a range of disciplines; Wolcott 2001 speaks to writing qualitative research more generally; Crang and Cook 2007 combines strategies for research and writing ethnography from the perspective of human geography; and Becker 1986/2007 is a classic for social science writing more generally. The sound advice for transforming a dissertation into a book in Luey 2004 is useful for ethnographically informed dissertations too.

Writers of creative nonfiction who have explored strategies for generating and shaping writing include Barrington 1997, Cheney 2001, Forché and Girard 2001, Gutkind 2005, and Talese and Lounsberry 1996. This larger movement is also described as "nonfiction" (Zinsser 2006) and "the fourth genre" (Root and Steinberg 2005). Journalists discuss "literary journalism" (Sims and Kramer 1995), the "New New Journalism" (Boynton 2005), and "narrative journalism" (Kramer and Call 2007). All these works, I think, are very relevant to ethnography. See Narayan 2007a for an earlier attempt to seek tools for ethnography from creative nonfiction, and Narayan 1999 for a yet earlier explanation of the border between ethnography and fiction.

I first encountered Chekhov's account of his trip to Sakhalin in a few pages from Chekhov 1967; I subsequently sought out other translations (Chekhov 2007 and the selections in Chekhov 2008). The stories and plays for which Chekhov is better known circulate in many translations and editions. For anyone seeking an introduction to his selected stories, I especially recommend Peavear and Volokhonsky's recent translations (Chekhov 2000, 2004). The notebook in which he recorded fragments of writing for future use is available too (Chekhov 1987), and I wish someone would translate this afresh. Several collections of his letters are available in English translation, each differently selected, organized, and edited, and I found them all worthwhile; see Chekhov 1920b, 1973, 2004a; Karlinsky 1975; McVay 1994; and, for his correspondence with Olga Knipper, Benedetti 1996. Especially when read in tandem with explanatory notes, these letters serve as Chekhov's unintended autobiography. Perhaps because Chekhov left such an enormous amount of writing, readers—including myself—often end up reading selectively, coming up with somewhat differing perceptions of his personality and his work.

Biographies of Chekhov that I've found particularly illuminating are Bartlett 2004, Chukovsky 1945, Coope 1997, Hingley 1976, and Rayfield 1997. In chapter 3, I quote from reminiscences written by a range of his contemporaries, though Janet Malcolm questions the factual value of these works. As she memorably writes, "The silence of the famous dead offers an enormous temptation to the self-promoting living. The opportunity to come out of the clammy void of obscurity and gain entrance into posterity's gorgeously lit drawing room through exaggerated claims of intimacy with one of the invited guests is hard to resist" (Malcolm 2001:79). See Bunin 2007, Gorky 1921, Gorky 1959:134–68, Katzer 1960, Koteliansky 1927, and Turkov 1990.

Many writers before me have been moved and inspired by Chekhov. When I began this book, I had already, a few years earlier, read and admired Malcolm's *Reading Chekhov: A Critical Journey* (2001), which weaves together her close and appreciative reading of Chekhov's stories, reflections on his life, and a narrative of her travels to places in Russia where Chekhov and his characters once lived. In the course of reading further, I savored other writers' accounts of how they savored his work: Vladimir Nabokov's chapter on Chekhov in *Lectures on Russian Literature* (1960/1981), James Wood's essay "What Chekhov Meant by Life" (1999), and Francine Prose's "What We Can Learn from Chekhov" (2006) are special delights. Two valuable anthologies in which writers and scholars join together to celebrate Chekhov are McConkey 1984 and Finke and Sherbinin 2007.

x freewriting. Elbow introduces this concept as follows: "The most effective way I know to improve your writing is to do freewriting exercises regularly. At least three times a week. They are sometimes called 'automatic writing,' 'babbling,' or 'jabbering' exercises. The idea is simply to write for ten minutes (later on, perhaps fifteen or twenty). Don't stop for anything. Go quickly without rushing. Never stop to look back, to cross something out, to wonder how to spell something, to wonder what word or thought to use, or to think about what you are doing. If you can't think of a word or a spelling, just use a squiggle or else write, 'I can't think of it.' Just put down something. . . . The only requirement is that you never stop" (1998:3).

xiii *I'm writing you this as a reader*. AC to Alexander Chekhov, Moscow, May 10, 1886 (McVay 1994:33). The entire letter is worth reading for Chekhov's advice on writing fiction, and especially on the use of tiny details to evoke larger scenes (using a beautiful image that he later attributed to the self-absorbed writer Trigorin in *The Seagull*).

1. STORY AND THEORY

1 *What are they like? Funny?* Chekhov 2004b:476.

2 *friendship, reason, progress, freedom*. Chekhov 2004b:477.

2 *writing culture*. See the influential *Writing Culture: The Poetics and Politics of Ethnography* (Clifford and Marcus 1986) and, for counterpoint, volumes like *Women Writing Culture* (Behar and Gordon 1995), *After Writing Culture* (James, Hockey, and Dawson 1997), and *Beyond Writing Culture* (Zenker and Kumoll, 2010).

2 *like an ethnologist, gravely and tediously*. Chekhov 1920a:91.

3 *scientific and literary purposes*. AC to M. N. Galkin-Vraskoy, Petersburg, January 20, 1890 (McVay 1994:84). On the question of contrary impulses in ethnography, I've found short articles by Robert Thornton (1983) and Barbara Tedlock (1991) to be especially helpful, along with the essays assembled in Clifford 1988.

5 *piles to files*. Thank you, Joel Score.

5 *creative nonfiction writers inform their readers*. Cheney 2001:2.

6 Seymour Glass. Salinger 1963:161.

7 *thick description*; example from Ryle. Geertz 1973:6–7.

8 stories as incipiently analytic. See especially Rosaldo 1989:127–43.

8 *fictions in the sense that*. Geertz 1973:15.

9 *what "faction"[is]*. Geertz 1988:141. Geertz has acknowledged the multiple genres in his own background, telling an interviewer that as an undergraduate at Antioch College, he wanted to be "a novelist and a newspaper man" and wrote an unpublished novel and short stories before shifting to philosophy and discovering anthropology (Olson 1991:189).

9 *the close-up; the long shot*. Barrington 1997:82. See also Cheney 2001. I also discuss some of these nonfiction tools for crafting ethnography in Narayan 2007a.

9 *Early in April of 1958*. Geertz 1973:414.

10 *In the midst of the third match*. Geertz 1973:414–15.

10 *to be teased is to be accepted*. Geertz 1973:416.

10–11 scenes with dramatic potential. Cheney 2001:55.

11 *I started from a real incident*. Wright, in Queneau 1958:15.

12 state violence in 1960s Indonesia. See George 2004.

12 *local events and local commentary; foreground preoccupations, background conditions*. Moore 1987:731. Keith Basso similarly describes his ethnographic practice as involving "the close contextualization of a handful of telling events" (1996:110), and Dwyer (1982) organizes his book around events and contextualizing dialogues.

13 *The situation is the context*. Gornick 2001:13. I am tempted to diverge from Gornick in seeing plot as part of the story. According to Gornick, a situation is effectively transformed into a story when a writer creates a particular persona. Looking through her favorite writers of personal essays and memoir, she finds, "In each case the writer was possessed of an insight that organized the writing, and in each case a persona had been created to serve the insight" (2001:23).

13 *Imagine yourself suddenly set down*. Malinowski 1922/1961:4.

14 *the native's point of view; We have to study man; the subjective desire of feeling*. Malinowski 1922/1961:21.

15 *ethnographies of the particular*. Abu-Lughod (1993) retells stories of Bedouin women's lives in the light of organizing structural principles, and argues for following particular people's lives as a way to write against assumptions of the "homogeneity, coherence and timelessness" associated with culture (1993:14). Also see Flueckiger on "the case for case studies" (2006:22).

15 *When you tell a story*. Narayan 1989:37. Also see Narayan and George 2000 on interviewing for stories and Jackson 2006 on the politics of storytelling.

15 *the moral significance of labor*. Chekhov 2004b:461.

15 *The question is not simply*. Strathern 1987:257.

18 *labels and tags as prejudices*. AC to A. N. Pleshcheyev (or Pleshcheev), Moscow, October 4, 1888 (Karlinsky 1975:109).

18 *chasing two hares; I feel more alert*. AC to A. Suvorin, Moscow, September 11, 1888 (Karlinksy 1975:107).

18 *The narrative form is a lawful wife*. AC to A. N. Pleshcheev, Moscow, January 15, 1889 (McVay 1994:72).

18 *I'm working on my Sakhalin book*. AC to M. V. Kiseleva, Bogimovo, May 20, 1891 (McVay 1994:109).

19 *Chekhov lent Kirin money*. Chukovsky 1945:24.

20 *Braz is painting my portrait*. to A. A. Khoytainsteva, Nice, March 23, 1898 (McVay 1994:196–97).

20 *solving a question; An artist observes*. AC to A. S. Suvorin, Moscow, October 27, 1888 (McVay 1994:61).

20 *New literary forms*. Chekhov 1987:28.

21 *nothing passes without a trace*. Chekhov 2004b:536.

21 *Life is given only once*. Chekhov 2004b:326. Malcolm quotes this same statement in a different translation: "Life is only given us once, and one wants to live it boldly, with full consciousness and beauty" (2001:135).

21 *To live simply to die*. Gorky 1959:164.

2. PLACE

23 *I saw everything; I don't know what I'll end up with*. AC to Suvorin, Tatar Strait, September 11, 1890 (Karlinsky 1975:171). Karlinsky explains the reference to Krylov. Even as Chekhov claims to be "done with the penal colony," further settlements awaited him in the south.

24 Chekhov's interest in Sakhalin. See Hingley 1976:128.

25 *at least one or two hundred pages; a place of unbearable suffering*. AC to A. Suvorin, Moscow, March 9, 1890 (Karlinksy 1975:159–60).

25 *I spend all day reading*. AC to A. N. Plescheev Moscow, February 15, 1890 (McVay 1994:85).

26 *Sakhalin Island* as ethnography. In "Chekhov as Ethnographer," the Slavic studies scholar Cathy Popkin argues that for Chekhov, stymied by the chaos on Sakhalin, "epistemological crisis leads to severe representational distress" (1992:45). She rounds up a wealth of documentation on how other scholars and writers have discussed Chekhov's book and concludes that it is "truly one of the strangest documents in any genre" (1992:48). The environmental and medical historian Conevery Bolton Valenčius (2007) helps clarify the book's strangeness by locating its form amid writings in the field of medical geography. See Ryfa 1999 for a further discussion of genre in the book, particularly the interweaving of travel, science, and literary discourses and the way that Chekhov is in dialogue with Dostoevsky, even as later Solzhenitsyn was in dialogue with Chekhov.

26 Ethnographers find the field. See Gupta and Ferguson 1997, Low and Lawrence-Zúñiga 2003. For more on multisited research, see Marcus 1998, Falzon 2009.

28 Drawing on the full range of senses. See Stoller 1989.

28 *"Passage to More Than India."* Singer 1972:11–38. Also see Said 1978 on Orientalism more generally.
29 "Sakhalin" as French misreading. Chekhov 2007:48.
29 *governors of Siberia*. Chekhov 2007:105. Also see Brunello and Lenček 2008: 94–95.
29 *Sizovskaya Street*. Chekhov 2007:151.
30 *Shades of Shit*. Basso 1996:24–27.
30 *Line of White Rocks*. Basso 1996:93–95.
30 *189 days with precipitation*. Chekhov 2007:110.
30 *It is high noon*. Mead 1928:20. Also see Shore 1982:5 and Taussig 2004:31–40 on heat.
31 *The temperature today felt cold*. Vitebsky 2005:154.
31 *The gutter trench*. Causey 2003:159.
32 *Now, the thick, damp air*. Causey 2003:159.
32 *far below the sensation*; *The days were sullen*. Causey 2003:160.
32 *the melancholy tuneful cries*. Gibbal 1994:11.
32 *little interior sea*. Gibbal 1994:13.
33 *the Niger widens*. Gibbal 1994:15.
33 *Every perspective requires a metaphor*. Burke and Gusfield 1989:95.
33 *Their eyes shine*. Briggs 1970:16.
34 *shape shifters of magnificent power*; *They respond to humans*. Cruikshank 2005:69.
34 *It was with Ma Salam*. Tsing 1993:66.
35 *An abandoned logging road*. Tsing 2005:29–30.
36 *transmigration villages*. Tsing 2005:30.
36 *Nowadays, in place of taiga*. Chekhov 2007:75.
37 *an irregular green ribbon*; *chimneys cast long shadows*; *the thatched roofs*; *But walking through a village*. Mintz 1974:12.
38 *The windows were open*; *There is no bedding*. Chekhov 2007:86.
39 *His sheepskin coat reeks*. Brunello and Lenček 2008:96–97.
40 *They have compassion*. AC to Nikolay Chekhov, Moscow, March 1886 (Chekhov 2004a:60).
40 *A discarded metal generator*. Bourgois and Schonberg 2009:3.
41 witness to a flogging. Chekhov 2007:291–94.
41 *blood spattered on the walls*; *They have asked us*. Das 2007:194.
42 *forced for the sake of a single mangy line*. AC to Suvorin, 27 May, 1891, Bogimovo (Cooke 1997:72).
42 *absence of lengthy verbiage*. AC to Alexander Chekhov (Karlinsky 1975:87).
43 *a department of ethnographical medicine*. Cited in Chukovsky 1945:42.
43 *Mattresses, old torn dressing gowns*; *a stench of pickled cabbage*. Chekhov 2000: 172, 173.
44 *Reassure your brother*. AC to David Manucharov, March 5, 1896, Melikhovo (Chekhov 2004a:341).

3. PERSON

45 *In Russia, no less than in our country*. Malcolm 2001:22.

47 "round" and "flat" characters. Forster 1927/1955:67–78.

48 *Krasivy Family-forgotten*. Chekhov 1967:45. In other translations the man appears as "Good looking Can't- remember-my-relations" (Chekhov 2007:78) and "Handsome Surname Forgotten" (Chekhov 2008:107). In *Sakhalin Island* and other Chekhov writings, I was troubled when I came across caricatures of women or minorities; yet the full body of his unfolding work and his actions appear to show his own growth past casual stereotypes and the prejudices of his times.

49 *each one, in itself*. Auster 1982/1988:28.

49 *The size of his hands*. Auster 1982/1988:29. Auster moves on to consider how a dramatic family secret might have shaped his father's isolation, his tentativeness, his unusual closeness to his own mother and brothers. Auster's generation learned of this secret only by chance, when a cousin sat on a plane next to someone who had grown up in the same town as Auster's father and siblings. Through newspaper clippings sent by this stranger, Auster was able to reconstruct the events that had irrevocably marked the lives in his Polish Jewish family when they lived in Wisconsin some forty years before.

50 *The iris of his right eye*. I take this detail from Alexander Kuprin (1927:44). Kuprin vehemently insists that though many recall Chekhov as having blue eyes, he actually had "dark, almost brown" eyes (other descriptions complicate this further by mentioning eyes that were hazel or gray). The famous painting of Chekhov by Braz shows brown eyes, as does his brother Nikolay's portrait of him.

51 *Anton Pavlovich's room*. Korovin 1990:16–17.

52 *growing weaker in health*. Knipper-Chekhova 1960:36.

52–53 *And he looked at us*. Knipper-Chekhova 1960:38. Chekhov wrote to Suvorin of how moved he was by Knipper's performance in a letter from Yalta, October 8, 1898 (McVay 1994:203–4).

53 *Antosha would sit at the table*. Kuprin 1927:62.

53 *His way of walking*. Cited in Hingley 1976:206–7.

54 *I recall how Taso looked*. Mintz 1974:3.

54 *it seemed strange to him*. Chekhov 2000:375.

55 *Time had sharpened his facial planes*. Myerhoff 1978:45.

55 *God's greatest invention*. Myerhoff 1978:69.

56 *The mind must be alive*. Myerhoff 1978:44.

56 *the work has no beginning*. Myerhoff 1978:47.

56 *like a fine cloak*. Myerhoff 1973:76.

57 *"From childhood, were you a devotee?"* Narayan 1989:48.

57–58 *swart elderly gnome; readily and at length*. Turner 1960:334.

58 *In the main, the pattern*. Turner 1960:343.

58 *In Chekhov's world*. Wood 1999:87–88. For the passage in "The Lady with the Little Dog" see Chekhov 2000:374. Also see Malcolm 2001:36–37.

59 *antonovska . . . antonovski*. This is mentioned by several authors; I noted it in McVay 1994:294.

59 *Evidently, his best time for work*. Kuprin 1927:60–61.

60 *I promise to be a splendid husband*. AC to Suvorin, March 23, 1895, Melikhovo (Chekhov 2004a:333). For a biography of Olga Knipper, see Pitcher 1979. The correspondence between Chekhov and Knipper (awkward to read, as other people's love letters usually are) is in Benedetti 1996.

60 *It's a long time since I drank champagne*. Knipper-Chekhova 1960:55. Malcolm lines up different retellings to show how this scene has become "one of the great set pieces in literary history" (2001:62).

61 *Her body shuddered and jerked*. Brown 1991:61.

62 *Watching old Spiridon rocking*. Willerslev 2007:1.

63 *I can imagine Makis*. Read 1965:16.

63 Loaded gun. Nemirovich-Danchenko 1990:92.

63 *I cannot explain why his image*. Nemirovich-Danchenko 1990: 91.

64 *expression either of guilt or of sympathy*. Chitau 1990:99.

4. VOICE

67 *He once invited me to visit him*. Gorky 1959:134–35. For a different translation, with a somewhat more mannered voice, see Gorky 1921:1. Chekhov's concern for other tubercular patients is also described in Chukovki 1945:28.

68 *This was often the way*. Gorky 1959:137.

69 Ethnography built from conversations. See especially Dwyer 1982; Tedlock and Mannheim 1995.

69 *You're like a spectator*. AC to M. Gorky, December 3, 1898, Yalta (McVay 1994:211).

69 *another piece of advice*. AC to M. Gorky, 3 September, 1899, Yalta (McVay 1994:236).

70 *The way he spoke*. Auster 1982/1988:29–30.

70 *deep, gentle, hushed voice*. Gorky 1959:139.

70 *a low bass with a deep metallic ring*. Nemirovich-Danchenko 1990:78.

70 *caressing baritone*. Soulerzhitsky 1927:171.

70 *leaning his head on his hand*. Knipper-Chekhova 1960:52.

71 *he laughed good-humouredly*. Stanislavski 1968:89.

71 *genuinely Russian*. Nemirovich-Danchenko 1990:78.

71 *In Neapolitan the voice is thick*. Belmonte 1979:5.

72 Thing *was the major abstract word*. Wolfe 1968:11.

74 *an explanation for tiredness*. Scheper-Hughes 1992:176–77.

74 *a lot of what is called* nervos. Scheper-Hughes 1992:177–78.

75 *somewhat inchoate, oblique*. Scheper-Hughes 1992:195.

75 For an example of a note on translation, see Narayan 1997:223–25.

76 *THOUGHTS ABOUT MY ACTIONS*. Dwyer 1982:225–26.

77 Time: *A late morning in March 1993*. Seizer 2005:1–2.

79 *He saw* **then** *that*. Tedlock 1993:182–83. Also see Tedlock 1983.
80 *As I undid necklaces of words*. Behar 1993:16. For more on life history as a genre, see Langness and Frank 1981.
81 *Yongsu's Mother's tales*. Kendall 1988:10–11.
81 *She fielded our queries*. Kendall 1988:18–19.
81 *Towards the end of my survey*. Stoller and Olkes 1987:9.
83 *often expressed his thought*. Stanislavki 1968:81.
83 *Then suddenly came the order*. Stanislavki 1968:113.
83 *I had heard many warnings; Someone in the village*. Vitebsky 2005:124.
84 *He took his gun to go hunting*. Abu-Lughod 1986:230–31.
86 *There are big dogs and little dogs*. Bunin 2007:20. This reference to howling reminds me of "Kashtanka," the dog who must howl every time she hears music, in Chekhov's story by that name (Pitcher 1999:86–104). Written from Kashtanka's perspective, the story shows up varied consequences of being compelled to howl in one's own voice.
86 *He had the ability; Love your heroes; Abandon "ready made-phrases."* Shchepkina-Kupernik 1990:59.
87 *wonderful things become even more wonderful; unrolling the pictures in my mind*. Dhar 2005:4.
87 *For me the act of singing*. Dhar 2005:5.
87 *you have first to listen to your own breath*. Dhar 2005:67.
88 *Take the note and with your breath*. Dhar 2005:66–67.
88 primly off-tune performance. Dhar 2005:97–98.
89 *Or in other words*. See Mills 1959; Narayan 2008.
90 *"word-in-the-street" language; managed to convey an impression*. Nabokov 1960/1981:252.
90 *By keeping all his words in the same dim light*. Nabokov 1960/1981:253.
90 *The story is told in the most natural way possible*. Nabokov 1960/1981:262.

5. SELF

95 Complete and uncensored letters. Bartlett 2004. McVay (1994) selects key lines from a range of letters for each year and also provides an overview of the entire extant correspondence for that year. For example, 203 letters written in 1891 have survived; of course, Chekhov could have written even more.
95 *In some respects, Chekhov's letters*. Bartlett 2004:xxxii.
95 *autobiographophobhia; Being forced to read*. AC to Gregory Rossilomo, October 11, 1899, Yalta (Bartlett 2004:424). Also see the earlier letters to Augustin Vrzal from Bogimovo, August 14, 1891, and to Vladimir Tikhonov in Moscow, February 22, 1892, that contain brief autobiographical statements.
95 *When I see books*. Chekhov 1987:20. This raises the question too of what's relevant about Chekhov's life when discussing his writing.
95 auto-ethnography. See especially Reed-Danahay 1997; Meneley and Young 2005. Aspects of the ethnographer's self may be revealed without adopting

the term "auto-ethnography," for example, in McLean and Leibing 2007; Collins and Gallinat 2010. For influential arguments in favor of working the self into any form of ethnographic writing, see Behar 1996; Dwyer 1982; Haraway 1988; Rosaldo 1989.

97 *Turning oneself into a character*. Lopate 2001:44.

97 *It was almost dusk when I left Noah*. Jackson 2004:10–11.

99 *I was glad when somebody told me*. Hurston 1978:3.

99 *"Well, if it ain't Zora Hurston!"; "Hello, heart-string."* Hurston 1978:34–35.

101 *I looked at the eyes around me*. Ghosh 1992:204.

101 *I sometimes wished I had told Nabeel*. Ghosh 1992:204–5.

102 *like a sloppily edited film*. Ghosh 1992:208.

102 *men dismembered for the state of their foreskins; I could not have expected them to understand*. Ghosh 1992:210.

103 *In Gurung villages, doorways are low*. McHugh 2001:29.

104 *It doesn't look good; From the time our children are small;She had been able to compare*. McHugh 2001:114.

105 *After two decades*. Khosravi 2010:22–23.

107 *hooted plaintively*. Chekhov 2004b:263.

107 *the same savage poverty and hunger; And he did not want to go home*. Chekhov 2004b:264.

108 *I picture it*. Chekhov 2004b:265.

108 *If the old woman wept; And joy suddenly stirred in his soul*. Chekhov 2004b:266.

WRITING TO BE ALIVE

112 *On Mondays, Tuesdays and Wednesdays*. AC to A. Suvorin, May 10, 1891,Aleksin (Chekhov 2004a:281–82).

112 *He rose at 4.00 a.m*. Rayfield 1997:248.

112 *I am bored, I am bored*. AC to A. Suvorin, August 28, 1891, Bogimovo (Chekhov 1920b:268).

112 *There are times*. AC to A. Suvorin, August 28, 1891, Bogimovo (Chekhov 1920b: 268–69).

112 *when I write nowadays*. AC to Lydia Avilova, July 26–27, 1898, Melikhovo (McVay 1994:199).

Readings and References

HELPFUL BOOKS ON WRITING

Many books carry wonderful advice on aspects of the writing process more generally, beyond ethnography. Here are a few books that I've found particularly encouraging and helpful through the years, as well as some recent discoveries. Even though I have not looked through all of my old favorites again to cite particular passages, they stand as a benevolent presence behind these pages.

Barrington, Judith. 1997. *Writing the Memoir: From Truth to Art*. Portland, OR: Eighth Mountain Press.

Brande, Dorothea. 1934. *Becoming a Writer*. New York: Harcourt, Brace & Co.

Cameron, Julia. 1992. *The Artist's Way: A Spiritual Path to Higher Creativity*. New York: Jeremy P. Tarcher.

Cheney, Theodore A. Rees. 2001. *Writing Creative Nonfiction: Fiction Techniques for Crafting Great Nonfiction*. Berkeley, CA: Ten Speed Press.

Forché, Carolyn, and Philip Gerard, eds. 2001. *Writing Creative Nonfiction: Instruction and Insights from Teachers of the Associated Writing Programs*. Cincinnati: Story Press.

Goldberg, Natalie. 1986. *Writing Down the Bones: Freeing the Writer Within*. Boston: Shambhala.

King, Stephen. 2002. *On Writing: A Memoir of the Craft*. New York: Scribner.

Kramer, Mark, and Wendy Call, eds. 2007. *Telling True Stories: A Nonfiction Writers' Guide from the Nieman Foundation at Harvard University*. New York: Plume.

Lamott, Anne. 1995. *Bird by Bird: Some Instructions on Writing and Life*. New York: Anchor.

Le Guin, Ursula K. 1998. *Steering the Craft: Exercises and Discussions on Story Writing for the Lone Navigator or the Mutinous Crew*. Portland, OR: Eighth Mountain Press.

Rilke, Rainer Maria. 1984. *Letters to a Young Poet*. Trans. Stephen Mitchell. New York: Random House.

Strunk, William, and E. B. White. 2005. *The Elements of Style*. New York: Penguin.

Ueland, Brenda. 1987. *If You Want to Write*. 2nd ed. Saint Paul, MN: Graywolf Press.

Zinsser, William Knowlton. 2006. *On Writing Well: The Classic Guide to Writing Nonfiction*. 30th anniversary ed. New York: HarperCollins.

WORKS CITED

Abu-Lughod, Lila. 1986. *Veiled Sentiments: Honor and Poetry in a Bedouin Society*. Berkeley: University of California Press.

———. 1993. *Writing Women's Worlds: Bedouin Stories*. Berkeley: University of California Press.

Agee, James, and Walker Evans. 1960. *Let Us Now Praise Famous Men: Three Tenant Families*. New York: Ballantine Books.

Angrosino, Michael V., ed. 2007. *Doing Cultural Anthropology: Projects for Ethnographic Data Collection*. Long Grove, IL: Waveland.

Auster, Paul. 1982/1988. *The Invention of Solitude*. New York: Penguin.

Barrington, Judith. 1997. *Writing the Memoir: From Truth to Art*. Portland, OR: Eighth Mountain Press.

Bartlett, Rosamund. 2004. *Chekhov: Scenes from a Life*. London: Free Press.

Basso, Keith H. 1996. *Wisdom Sits in Places: Landscape and Language among the Western Apache*. Albuquerque: University of New Mexico Press.

Becker, Howard. 1986/2007. *Writing for Social Scientists: How to Start and Finish Your Thesis, Book, or Article*. With a chapter by Pamela Richards. 2nd ed. Chicago: University of Chicago Press.

———. 2007. *Telling about Society*. Chicago: University of Chicago Press.

Behar, Ruth. 1993. *Translated Woman: Crossing the Border with Esperanza's Story*. Boston: Beacon Press.

———. 1996. *The Vulnerable Observer: Anthropology That Breaks Your Heart*. Boston: Beacon Press.

Behar, Ruth, and Deborah A. Gordon, eds. 1995. *Women Writing Culture*. Berkeley: University of California Press.

Belmonte, Thomas. 1979. *The Broken Fountain*. New York: Columbia University Press.

Benedetti, Jean. 1996. *Dear Writer— Dear Actress— The Love Letters of Olga Knipper and Anton Chekhov*. London: Methuen Drama.

Bourgois, Philippe, and Jeff Schonberg. 2009. *Righteous Dopefiend*. Berkeley: University of California Press.

Boynton, Robert S. 2005. *The New New Journalism: Conversations with America's Best Nonfiction Writers on Their Craft*. New York: Vintage.

Brown, Karen McCarthy. 1991. *Mama Lola: A Vodou Priestess in Brooklyn*. Berkeley: University of California Press.

Bunin, Ivan A. 2007. *About Chekhov: The Unfinished Symphony*. Trans. and ed. Thomas Gaiton Marullo. Evanston, IL: Northwestern University Press.

Burke, Kenneth, and Joseph R. Gusfield. 1989. *On Symbols and Society*. Chicago: University of Chicago Press.

Causey, Andrew. 2003. *Hard Bargaining in Sumatra: Western Travelers and Toba Bataks in the Marketplace of Souvenirs*. Honolulu: University of Hawai'i Press.

Chekhov, Anton Pavlovich. 1920a. *The Chorus Girl and Other Stories*. Trans. Constance Garnett. New York: Macmillan.

———. 1920b. *Letters of Anton Chekhov to His Family and Friends, with Biographical Sketch*. Trans. and ed. Constance Garnett. New York: Macmillan.

———. 1967. *The Island: A Journey to Sakhalin*. Trans. Luba and Michael Terpak. New York: Washington Square Press.

———. 1973. *Letters of Anton Chekhov*. Ed. Avrahm Yarmolinsky. New York: Viking.

———. 1987. *Notebook of Anton Chekhov*. Trans. S. S. Koteliansky and Leonard Woolf. New York: Ecco Press.

———. 2000. *Stories*. Trans. Richard Pevear and Larissa Volokhonsky. New York: Bantam Books.

———. 2004a. *Anton Chekhov: A Life in Letters*. Trans. and ed. Rosamund Bartlett. London: Penguin.

———. 2004b. *The Complete Short Novels*. Trans. Richard Pevear and Larissa Volokhonsky. New York: Everyman's Library.

———. 2007. *Sakhalin Island*. Trans. Brian Reeve. Oxford: Oneworld Classics.

———. 2008. *How to Write Like Chekhov: Advice and Inspiration, Straight from His Own Letters and Work*. Ed. Piero Brunello and Lena Lenček. Trans. Lena Lenček. Cambridge, MA: Da Capo Lifelong.

Cheney, Theodore A. Rees. 2001. *Writing Creative Nonfiction: Fiction Techniques for Crafting Great Nonfiction*. Berkeley, CA: Ten Speed Press.

Chitau, M. M. 1990. "The Premiere of *The Seagull* (Reminiscences)." In *Anton Chekhov and His Times*, ed. Andrei M. Turkov, 94–99. Trans. Cynthia Carlile. Moscow: Progress Publishers.

Chukovsky, Kornei. 1945. *Chekhov the Man*. Trans. Pauline Rose. London: Hutchinson.

Clifford, James. 1988. *The Predicament of Culture: Twentieth-Century Ethnography, Literature, and Art*. Cambridge, MA: Harvard University Press.

Clifford, James, and George Marcus, eds. 1986. *Writing Culture: The Poetics and Politics of Ethnography*. Berkeley: University of California Press.

Collins, Peter, and Anselma Gallinat, eds. 2010. *The Ethnographic Self as Resource: Writing Memory and Experience into Ethnography*. New York: Berghahn Books.

Coope, John. 1997. *Doctor Chekhov: A Study in Literature and Medicine*. Chale: Cross Publishing.

Crang, Mike, and Ian Cook. 2007. *Doing Ethnographies*. Los Angeles: Sage.

Cruikshank, Julie. 2005. *Do Glaciers Listen? Local Knowledge, Colonial Encounters, and Social Imagination*. Vancouver: University of British Columbia Press; Seattle: University of Washington Press.

Das, Veena. 2007. *Life and Words: Violence and the Descent into the Ordinary*. Berkeley: University of California Press.

Davies, Charlotte Aull. 2002. *Reflexive Ethnography: A Guide to Research*. New York: Routledge.

Dhar, Sheila. 2005. *Raga'n Josh: Stories from a Musical Life*. New Delhi: Permanent Black.

Dwyer, Kevin. 1982. *Moroccan Dialogues: Anthropology in Question*. Baltimore: Johns Hopkins University Press.

Elbow, Peter. 1998. *Writing without Teachers*. 25th anniversary ed. New York: Oxford University Press.

Ellen, Roy, ed. 1984. *Ethnographic Research: A Guide to General Conduct*. London: Academic Press.

Emerson, Robert M., Rachel I. Fretz, and Linda L. Shaw. 1995. *Writing Ethnographic Fieldnotes*. Chicago: University of Chicago Press.

Finke, Michael C., and Julie de Sherbinin, eds. 2007. *Chekhov the Immigrant: Translating a Cultural Icon*. Bloomington, IN: Slavica Publishers.

Flueckiger, Joyce Burkhalter. 2006. *In Amma's Healing Room: Gender and Vernacular Islam in South India*. Bloomington: Indiana University Press.

Forché, Carolyn, and Philip Gerard, eds. 2001. *Writing Creative Nonfiction: Instruction and Insights from Teachers of the Associated Writing Programs*. Cincinnati: Story Press.

Forster, E. M. 1927/1955. *Aspects of the Novel*. New York: Harcourt, Brace & Company.

Gay y Blasco, Paloma, and Huon Wardle. 2007. *How to Read Ethnography*. London: Routledge.

Geertz, Clifford. 1973. *The Interpretation of Cultures: Selected Essays*. New York: Basic Books.

———. 1983. *Local Knowledge: Further Essays in Interpretive Anthropology*. New York: Basic Books.

———. 1988. *Works and Lives: The Anthropologist as Author*. Stanford, CA: Stanford University Press.

George, Kenneth M. 2004. "Violence, Culture, and the Indonesian Public Sphere: Reworking the Geertzian Legacy." In *Violence: Culture, Performance and Expression*, ed. Neil L. Whitehead, 25–54. Santa Fe: SAR Press.

Ghosh, Amitav. 1989. *The Shadow Lines*. New York: Viking.

———. 1992. *In an Antique Land: History in the Guise of a Traveler's Tale*. London: Granta Books/Penguin.

Gibbal, Jean-Marie. 1994. *Genii of the River Niger*. Trans. Beth G. Raps. Chicago: University of Chicago Press.

Goldenveizer, A. B. 2006. *Talks with Tolstoi*. In *Translations from the* Russian. Trans. Virginia Woolf and S. S. Koteliansky, 181–290. Southport: Virginia Woolf Society of Great Britain.

Gorky, Maxim. 1921. "Fragments of Recollections." In *Reminiscences of Anton Chekhov*. Trans. S. S. Koteliansky and Leonard Woolf, 1–28. New York: B. W. Huebsch.

———. 1959. *Literary Portraits*. Trans. Ivy Litvinov. Moscow: Foreign Languages Publishing House.

Gornick, Vivian. 2001. *The Situation and the Story: The Art of Personal Narrative*. New York: Farrar, Straus and Giroux.

Gupta, Akhil, and James Ferguson, eds. 1997. *Anthropological Locations: Boundaries and Grounds of a Field Science*. Berkeley: University of California Press.

Gutkind, Lee, ed. 2005. *In Fact: The Best of Creative Nonfiction*. New York: W. W. Norton.

Haraway, Donna. 1988. "Situated Knowledges: The Science Question in Feminism and the Privilege of Partial Perspective." *Feminist Studies* 14:575–99.

Hingley, Ronald. 1976. *A New Life of Anton Chekhov*. New York: Knopf.

Hurston, Zora Neale. 1978. *Mules and Men*. Bloomington: Indiana University Press.

Jackson, Bruce, and Edward D. Ives, eds. 1996. *The World Observed: Reflections on the Fieldwork Process*. Urbana: University of Illinois Press.

Jackson, Michael. 1989. *Paths towards a Clearing: Radical Empiricism and Ethnographic Inquiry*. Bloomington: Indiana University Press.

———. 2004. *In Sierra Leone*. Durham, NC: Duke University Press.

———. 2006. *The Politics of Storytelling: Violence, Transgression and Intersubjectivity*. Copenhagen: Museum Tusculanum Press.

James, Allison, Jenny Hockey, and Andrew Dawson, eds. 1997. *After Writing Culture: Epistemology and Praxis in Contemporary Anthropology*. London: Routledge.

Karlinsky, Simon. 1975. *Anton Chekhov's Life and Thought: Selected Letters and Commentary*. Trans. Michael Henry Heim with Simon Karlinsky. Berkeley: University of California Press.

Kendall, Laurel. 1988. *The Life and Hard Times of a Korean Shaman: Of Tales and the Telling of Tales*. Honolulu: University of Hawai'i Press.

Khosravi, Shahram. 2010. *"Illegal" Traveller: An Auto-Ethnography of Borders*. Basingstoke: Palgrave Macmillan.

Knipper-Chekhova, Olga. 1960. "The Last Years." In *A. P. Chekhov: 1860–1960*, ed. Julius Katzer, 31–55. Moscow: Foreign Languages Publishing House.

Korovin, K. A. 1990. "From My Meetings with Anton Chekhov." In *Anton Chekhov and His Times*, ed. Andrei M. Turkov, 16–23. Trans. Cynthia Carlile. Moscow: Progress Publishers.

Koteliansky, Samuel S., trans. and ed. 1927. *Anton Tchekhov: Literary and Theatrical Reminiscences*. New York: G. H. Doran.

Kramer, Mark, and Wendy Call, eds. 2007. *Telling True Stories: A Nonfiction Writers' Guide from the Nieman Foundation at Harvard University*. New York: Plume.

Kuprin, Alexander. 1927. "To Chekhov's Memory." In *Reminiscences of Anton Chekhov*. Trans. S. S. Koteliansky and Leonard Woolf, 29–90. New York: B. W. Huebsch.

Langness, L. L., and Gelya Frank. 1981. *Lives: An Anthropological Approach to Biography*. Novato, CA: Chandler & Sharp.

Lassiter, Luke E. 2005. *The Chicago Guide to Collaborative Ethnography*. Chicago: University of Chicago Press.

Lopate, Philip. 2001. "Writing Personal Essays: On the Necessity of Turning Oneself into a Character." In *Writing Creative Nonfiction: Instruction and Insights from Teachers of the Associated Writing Programs*, ed. Carolyn Forché and Philip Gerard, 38–44. Cincinnati: Story Press.

Low, Setha M., and Denise Lawrence-Zúñiga, eds. 2003. *The Anthropology of Space and Place: Locating Culture*. Malden, MA: Blackwell.

Luey, Beth, ed. 2004. *Revising Your Dissertation: Advice from Leading Editors*. Berkeley: University of California Press.

Malcolm, Janet. 2001. *Reading Chekhov: A Critical Journey*. New York: Random House.

Malinowski, Bronislaw. 1922/1961. *Argonauts of the Western Pacific: An Account of Native Enterprise and Adventure in the Archipelagoes of Melanesian New Guinea*. London: George Routledge & Sons.

Marcus, George E. 1998. *Ethnography through Thick and Thin*. Princeton, NJ: Princeton University Press.

Marcus, George E., and Michael M. J. Fischer. 1999. *Anthropology as Cultural Critique: An Experimental Moment in the Human Sciences*. 2nd ed. Chicago: University of Chicago Press.

McConkey, James, ed. 1984 *Chekhov and Our Age. Responses to Chekhov by American Writers and Scholars*. Ithaca, NY: Cornell University Center for International Studies.

McHugh, Ernestine. 2001. *Love and Honor in the Himalayas: Coming to Know Another Culture*. Philadelphia: University of Pennsylvania Press.

McLean, Athena, and Annette Leibing, eds. 2007. *The Shadow Side of Fieldwork: Exploring the Blurred Borders between Ethnography and Life*. Malden, MA: Blackwell.

McVay, Gordon, trans. and ed. 1994. *Chekhov: A Life in Letters*. London: Folio Society.

Mead, Margaret. 1928. *Coming of Age in Samoa: A Psychological Study of Primitive Youth for Western Civilization*. New York: W. Morrow & Co.

Meneley, Anne, and Donna Jean Young, eds. 2005. *Auto-Ethnographies: The Anthropology of Academic Practices*. Peterborough, ON: Broadview Press.

Mills, C. Wright. 1959. *The Sociological Imagination*. New York: Oxford University Press.

Mintz, Sidney W. 1974. *Worker in the Cane: A Puerto Rican Life History*. New Haven, CT: Yale University Press.

Mulcahy, Joanne. 2010. *Remedios: The Healing Life of Eva Castellanoz*. San Antonio, TX: Trinity University Press.

Myerhoff, Barbara. 1978. *Number Our Days*. New York: Dutton.

Nabokov, Vladimir. 1960/1981. *Lectures on Russian Literature*. Ed. Fredson Bowers. London: Pan Books.

Narayan, Kirin. 1989. *Storytellers, Saints, and Scoundrels: Folk Narrative in Hindu Religious Teaching*. Philadelphia: University of Pennsylvania Press.

———. 1997. *Mondays on the Dark Night of the Moon: Himalayan Foothill Folktales*. In collaboration with Urmila Devi Sood. New York: Oxford University Press.

———. 1999. "Ethnography and Fiction: Mapping a Border." *Anthropology and Humanism* 24:1–14.

———. 2007a. "Tools to Shape Texts: What Creative Nonfiction Can Offer Ethnography." *Anthropology and Humanism* 32 (2): 130–44.

———. 2007b. *My Family and Other Saints*. Chicago: University of Chicago Press.

———. 2008. "'Or in Other Words': Recasting Grand Theory." *Journal of Folklore Research* 45 (1): 83–90.

Narayan, Kirin, and Kenneth M. George. 2000. "Interviewing for Folk and Personal Narrative." In *Handbook of Interview Research*, ed. Jay Gubrium and James Holstein, 815–31. New York: Sage.

Nemirovich-Danchenko, V. I. 1990. "Chekhov." In *Anton Chekhov and His Times*, ed. Andrei M. Turkov, 74–93. Trans. Cynthia Carlile. Moscow: Progress Publishers.

Olson, Gary. 1991. "The Social Scientist as Author: Clifford Geertz on Ethnography and Social Construction." In *(Inter)views: Cross-Discplinary Perspectives on Rhetoric and Literacy*, ed. Gary A. Olson and Irene Gale, 187–210. Cabondale: Southern Illinois State Press.

Pitcher, Harvey. 1979. *Chekhov's Leading Lady: A Portrait of the Actress Olga Knipper*. London: John Murray.

———. 1999. *Chekhov: The Comic Stories*. Chicago: Ivan R. Dee.

Popkin, Cathy. 1992. "Chekhov as Ethnographer: Epistemological Crisis on Sakhalin Island." *Slavic Review* 51 (1): 36–51.

Prose, Francine. 2006. "What We Can Learn from Chekhov." In *Reading Like a Writer: A Guide for People Who Love Books and for Those Who Want to Write Them*, 233–48. New York: HarperCollins.

Queneau, Raymond. 1958. *Exercises in Style*. Trans. with an introduction by Barbara Wright. London: Gaberbocchus.

Rayfield, Donald. 1997. *Anton Chekhov: A Life*. New York: Henry Holt.

Read, Kenneth E. 1965. *The High Valley*. New York: Scribner.

Reed-Danahay, Deborah, ed. 1997. *Auto/ethnography: Rewriting the Self and the Social*. Oxford: Berg.

Robben, Antonius, C. G. M., and Jeffrey A. Sluka, eds. 2007. *Ethnographic Fieldwork: An Anthropological Reader*. Malden, MA: Blackwell.

Root, Robert L., and Michael Steinberg, eds. 2005. *The Fourth Genre: Contemporary Writers of/on Creative Nonfiction*. New York: Pearson Longman.

Rosaldo, Renato. 1989. *Culture and Truth: The Remaking of Social Analysis*. Boston: Beacon Press.

Ryfa, Juras T. 1999. *The Problem of Genre and the Quest for Justice in Chekhov's The Island of Sakhalin*. Studies in Slavic Languages and Literature, vol. 13. Lewiston, NY: Edwin Mellen Press.

Said, Edward. 1978. *Orientalism*. New York: Pantheon.

Salinger, J. D. 1963. *Raise High the Roof Beam, Carpenters*, and *Seymour—An Introduction*. Boston: Little, Brown.

Scheper-Hughes, Nancy. 1992. *Death without Weeping: The Violence of Everyday Life in Brazil*. Berkeley: University of California Press.

Seizer, Susan. 2005. *Stigmas of the Tamil Stage: An Ethnography of Special Drama Artists in South India*. Durham, NC: Duke University Press.

Sharman, Russell Leigh, ed. 2007. "The Art of Ethnography: Narrative Style as a Research Method." Special issue. *Anthropology and Humanism* 32.

Shchepkina-Kupernik, T. L. 1990. "On Chekhov." In *Anton Chekhov and His Times*, ed. Andrei M. Turkov, 38–73. Trans. Cynthia Carlile. Moscow: Progress Publishers.

Shore, Bradd. 1982. *Sala'ilua, a Samoan Mystery*. New York: Columbia University Press.

Sims, Norman, and Mark Kramer, eds. 1995. *Literary Journalism: A New Collection of the Best American Nonfiction*. New York: Ballantine Books.

Singer, Milton B. 1972. "Passage to More Than India." In *When a Great Tradition Modernizes: An Anthropological Approach to Indian Civilization*, 11–38. New York: Praeger.

Soulerzhitsky, L. A. 1927. "Reminiscences by Mme. M. P. Lilin." In *Anton Tchekhov: Literary and Theatrical Reminiscences*. Trans. and ed. S. S. Koteliansky, 170–71. New York: G. H. Doran.

Stanislavski, Constantin. 1968. *Stanislavski's Legacy*. Trans. and ed. Elizabeth Reynolds Hapgood. London: Methuen.

Stoller, Paul. 1989. *The Taste of Ethnographic Things: The Senses in Anthropology*. Philadelphia: University of Pennsylvania Press.

Stoller, Paul, and Cheryl Olkes. 1987. *In Sorcery's Shadow: A Memoir of Apprenticeship among the Songhay of Niger*. Chicago: University of Chicago Press.

Strathern, Marilyn. 1987. "Out of Context: The Persuasive Fictions of Anthropology." *Current Anthropology* 28 (3): 251–81.

Sunstein, Bonnie Stone, and Elizabeth Chiseri-Strater. 2002. *FieldWorking: Reading and Writing Research*. 2nd ed. Boston: Bedford/St. Martin's.

Talese, Gay, and Barbara Lounsberry, eds. 1996. *Writing Creative Nonfiction: The Literature of Reality*. New York: HarperCollins College.

Taussig, Michael. 2004. *My Cocaine Museum*. Chicago: University of Chicago Press.

Tedlock, Barbara. 1991. "From Participant Observation to the Observation of Participation: The Emergence of Narrative Ethnography." *Journal of Anthropological Research* 47:69–94.

Tedlock, Dennis. 1983. *The Spoken Word and the Work of Interpretation*. Philadelphia: University of Pennsylvania Press.

———. 1993. *Breath on the Mirror: Mythic Voices and Visions of the Living Maya*. San Francisco: Harper.

Tedlock, Dennis, and Bruce Mannheim, eds. 1995. *The Dialogic Emergence of Culture*. Urbana: University of Illinois Press.

Thornton, Robert J. 1983. "Narrative Ethnography in Africa, 1850–1920: The Creation and Capture of an Appropriate Domain for Anthropology." *Man* 18:502–20.

Tsing, Anna Lowenhaupt. 1993. *In the Realm of the Diamond Queen: Marginality in an Out-of-the-Way Place*. Princeton, NJ: Princeton University Press.

———. 2005. *Friction: An Ethnography of Global Connection*. Princeton, NJ: Princeton University Press.

Turkov, Andrei M., ed. 1990. *Anton Chekhov and His Times*. Trans. Cynthia Carlile and Sharon McKee. Moscow: Progress Publishers.

Turner, Victor. 1960. "Muchona the Hornet, Interpreter of Religion." In *In the Company of Man: Twenty Portraits by Anthropologists*, ed. Joseph B. Casagrande, 334–55. New York: Harper.

Valenčius, Conevery Bolton. 2007. "Chekhov's Sakhalin Island and Medical Geography." In *Chekhov the Immigrant: Translating a Cultural Icon*, ed. Michael C. Finke and Julie W. De Sherbinin, 299–314. Bloomington, IN: Slavica Publishers.

Van Maanen, John. 1988. *Tales of the Field: On Writing Ethnography*. Chicago: University of Chicago Press.

Vitebsky, Piers. 2005. *The Reindeer People: Living with Animals and Spirits in Siberia*. Boston: Houghton Mifflin.

Waterston, Alisse, and Maria D. Vesperi, eds. 2009. *Anthropology Off the Shelf: Anthropologists on Writing*. Malden, MA: Wiley Blackwell.

Willerslev, Rane. 2007. *Soul Hunters: Hunting, Animism, and Personhood among the Siberian Yukaghirs*. Berkeley: University of California Press.

Wolf, Margery. 1992. *A Thrice-Told Tale: Feminism, Postmodernism and Ethnographic Responsibility*. Stanford, CA: Stanford University Press.

Wolfe, Tom. 1968. *The Electric Kool-Aid Acid Test*. New York: Farrar, Strauss and Giroux.

Wolcott, Harry F. 2001. *Writing Up Qualitative Research*. 2nd ed. Thousand Oaks, CA: Sage.

Wood, James. 1999. "What Chekhov Meant by Life." In *The Broken Estate: Essays on Literature and Belief*, 74–88. New York: Random House.

Index

Lightning Source UK Ltd.
Milton Keynes UK
UKHW011044120719
346000UK00001B/5/P